Once a Boy

by

Paul Gardner

Published by

Mystic Dragon Publishing

3519 Cosbey Avenue

Baldwin Park, Ca 91706

ISBN: 978-1-7367705-3-5 (hc)

ISBN: 978-1-7367705-4-2 (sc)

ISBN: 978-1-7367705-5-9 (e)

LCCN: 2021913195

Cover Art by Sam Villareale

DISCLAIMER

I was born Paul Gardner Mittelstaedt in Sanborn, New York, on April 8, 1947, to Paul and Helen Mittelstaedt. Until 1974, my name was Paul Mittelstaedt. I legally dropped my last name because I got tired of spelling it three times every time I said it once.

In the process of recollecting experiences for the purposes of this memoir, I struggled with remembering names. Because we often called each other nicknames, it was not always possible to identify or locate an individual using their nickname. My nickname was Mitt. Lt. Rich somehow heard it as Mick, and so it was for the rest of my tour. Some of those to whom I did give names are only identified with part of their names, owing in part to the need to ask them first for permission to use their names.

Furthermore, some of the Vietnam vets have passed away since most of us are well into our seventies. When I enlisted in the United States Army on April 11, 1966, I had just turned nineteen. Young, invincible, and looking for adventure—this is my story. The draft was looming large and I wanted choices. So, I made the choice to enlist, and I have no regrets and am proud of my service to our country.

Disclaimers turn up everywhere in today's environment. You can't open a peanut butter jar without reading one. So here's mine. The names you see may or may not be their real names. In certain cases I did use whole or parts of the names so that when I wrote about them, I would see their faces.

CONTENTS

CONTENTS (cont'd)

FOREWORD

Stateside: August 1967

The Political Front:

Politically, the Johnson administration had escalated the war in 1964, having vowed not to lose to the Communist North Vietnamese. President Lyndon Johnson ordered an increase of sustained bombing in the north (Operation Rolling Thunder) and expanded troop deployment. His decision to escalate the war caused his popularity to plummet. By 1967, Johnson's deepening commitment to an expanded military campaign (requiring Congressional appropriations to provide support and funding to South Vietnam) brought further criticism from anti-war demonstrators. By 1968, Johnson decided to step away from the office of presidency, refusing to run for reelection. In his mind, Vietnam was a war that he could neither abandon nor likely win.

The Media and Rise of Anti-war Sentiments

Back in the U.S., ten thousand miles away from the highlands of Vietnam where Paul was stationed, his buddies who were deferred from the draft were "Groovin' on a Sunday afternoon" and "Feelin' All Right," listening to "Happy Together" and hugging their young loves at the drive-in theater.

The media was looking for an end to the war, and so they purposely worded stories to fit that message. Meanwhile, as the military became increasingly displeased with the reporting, American citizens back home witnessed scenes of violent engagements, demoralized soldiers, and a losing war. As a result, anti-war sentiments soon skyrocketed.

The public kept themselves distracted from the war while watching *Andy Griffith, Gunsmoke, Bonanza, The Beverly Hillbillies.* Even *Gomer Pyle: U.S.M.C.*, a hayseed comedy series about Marine recruits at bootcamp, made not a single reference to the war that was going on in Vietnam.

Others back home were being swept up by a countercultural revolution, smoking pot, dropping acid, demonstrating against the Vietnam War and listening to "White Rabbit," "Born to Be Wild," and "All You Need is Love." What a juxtaposition.

At the Monterey Pop Festival in 1967, Country Joe and the Fish sang about going to fight in Vietnam and what would become an anti-war anthem: "Put down your books and pick up a gun, we're gonna' have a whole lot of fun." ("I Feel Like I'm Fixin' to Die Rag")

Social tumult and angst were the order of the day in the late '60s. Every evening Walter Cronkite and *CBS Evening News* brought the reality of war into American living rooms, documenting death and destruction from the jungles, highlands, and rice patties of Vietnam. "To say that we are mired in stalemate seems the only realistic, yet unsatisfactory, conclusion."

For the first time television brought the horrors of war into the living room. Vietnam may have been in Southeast Asia, but half the fighting occurred in the United States because journalists in Vietnam brought a different, pragmatic view to the American public than what the government was providing. On November 21, General Westmoreland reported: "I am absolutely certain that whereas in 1965 the enemy was winning, today he is certainly losing."

Westmoreland's misleading optimism and, in some cases, outright deception soon ignited an anti-war movement previously unseen on American soil. The White House stipulated a policy of "minimum candor"—censorship in effect. Failed military strategies would be relegated to the classified files not the CBS news. In the end, though, the policy damaged public trust and credibility, and soon support of the Johnson administration began waning.

A major development that swayed public support away from the war effort came when Walter Cronkite delivered his famous anti-war opinion on-air during his CBS broadcast in February 27, 1968. The report came just after the Tet Offensive. Having recently returned from reporting overseas, Cronkite began his broadcast by saying, "Tonight, back in more familiar surroundings in New York, we'd like to sum up our findings in Vietnam, an analysis that must be speculative, personal, and subjective. To say that we are mired in stalemate seems the only realistic, yet unsatisfactory, conclusion. It is clear to this reporter that the only rational way out then will be to negotiate, not as victors, but as an honorable people who lived up to their pledge to defend democracy, and did the best they could."

Four years after the assassination of JFK, the *Warren Report* and countless conspiracy theories about his death flooded bookstores. For many Americans, the true cause of President Kennedy's death was still in doubt and still lingered in their minds. In September of 1963, just two months before the assassination, President Kennedy felt that unless the South Vietnamese provided more support, the war could not be won. "It's their war. They're the ones who have to win it or lose it."

In the long, hot summer of '67 a different kind of war was raging in more than a hundred cities across the U.S. Racial violence flared, with at least 177 persons killed and thousands injured in riots. National Guard troops rushed onto the city streets of Newark and other cities to put an end to looting and violence. Property damage approached one billion dollars.

Anti-war sentiments grew, and soon the mounting discontent started to boil. Give up or charge ahead? Escalate or de-escalate? Americans began to question the humanity of war. The controversial raid on Hamburger Hill raised questions about the futility of fighting to take over a hill that was later considered strategically unnecessary and of no military value. Seventy-two soldiers died and 372 wounded.

The death toll of enemy soldiers (NVA) lost in the battle was 633. The public began to seriously question the logic of the military's tactical operations. Though the Hamburger Hill losses were much smaller than the enemy's, they set off a firestorm of protest back home. The American people were growing weary of the war. A February 1969 poll revealed that only 39 percent still supported the war, while 52 percent believed sending troops to fight in Vietnam had been a mistake.

Understandably, there was great resentment between those men serving in Vietnam and those "draft-dodger" brothers back Stateside marching in anti-war demonstrations. Troops listened to the anti-war songs on the radio, and when in 1969 John Fogerty, leader of Credence Clearwater Revival, wrote the song "Fortunate Son," many men of draftable age were thinking of ways to win a deferment to avoid serving in Vietnam. Unlike previous twentieth-century conflicts, it seemed like the government was handing out exemptions and delays to anyone with the resources to meet the low standards for getting one. In sharp contrast to World War II when over half of eligible men served, we went from an era where every single family had a direct connection to the risk and sacrifice of the war to one where children of privilege could dodge that responsibility. For those enlisted men fighting for freedom and doing their best to survive a brutal war, the privileged young men who could buy their way out of service caused great bitterness, feelings of abandonment, and lowered morale.

Paul's moving story of his service in Vietnam in the late'60s is one of innocence, bravery, service and survival. Paul, like many of his young enlisted brothers, went off to war in the hopes of fighting for South Vietnam's freedom from Communist aggression from the north. Soon after being deployed to a strange far-off land ten thousand miles from his home in Rochester, New York, Paul's military engagement would throw him into the intense combat zone as a gunship gunner. As if survival in this deadly arena of war was not enough of a challenge for a young and inexperienced twenty-year-old soldier, the anti-war demonstrations and political turmoil back home did little to buoy his morale. To fully appreciate his experiences in the war in Vietnam is to understand the political and cultural upheaval that took place in his homeland.

Aftermath:

Vietnam veterans have long been viewed as damaged goods. The public's negative view of Vietnam veterans who had fought in what many Americans perceived as an unjust war fostered a stigma that could not be shaken. More than 300,000 American soldiers were likely wounded physically from high war-zone exposure. Paul Gardner was one of the many wounded, having suffered a serious and disabling shrapnel injury during a mortar attack.

More than half of the veterans required hospitalization, and approximately one quarter (more than 75,000) became seriously disabled. Vietnam veterans had experienced clinically trauma-induced symptoms apart from their physical wounds in relation to their war-zone combat experiences much like the portrayal of the protagonists portrayed in the films *Coming Home* and *Born on the Fourth of July*.

The stigma of veterans as damaged goods persisted long after the war. Perhaps even more commonly, they were assumed to be scarred psychologically from the trauma of war-zone exposure, much like the men returning from war in *The Deer Hunter*, who played Russian roulette as a sign of their alienation. At the time, PTSD (Post-traumatic Stress Disorder) was referred to as *Gross Stress Reaction*. It was not until the 1980s (after Desert Storm) that the term PTSD came into clinical and lay-accepted usage.

In general, veterans were woefully neglected by the government. Veterans received far less generous benefits than their forebears who served in World War II. GI benefits available for Vietnam veterans were almost nonexistent. Veterans did benefit from higher earnings, as well as lower inequality if they served during the World War II era, and to some extent the decade immediately after that war. They began to suffer lower earnings if they served in the Vietnam War and the decade following the end of that conflict.

As more and more wartime atrocities came to light (My Lai massacre, Tiger Force, rogue GI's, etc.), there was a national implication of guilt and shame placed on Vietnam veterans as participants in a brutal, unsuccessful war. The stereotype of the broken, homeless Vietnam vet began to take hold. It would take nearly twenty years after the end of the war for America give proper respect to its Vietnam veterans. The dedication of the Vietnam Veterans Memorial in 1982 began the process, and the Gulf War of 1990-91helped to put an end to the *Vietnam Syndrome*.

The incidence of alcoholism and drug abuse was high among soldiers while stationed in Vietnam. After returning home, veterans suffering from crippling physical injuries and the late and delayed effects of combat exposure in the form of PTSD often sought comfort with alcohol and drug abuse. As a result, an ongoing (chronic) traumatic-stress syndrome included many or even all of the following behaviors: depressive episodes, panic disorder, obsessive disorder, generalized anxiety disorder, alcohol abuse/dependence, substance abuse/dependence, and antisocial personality disorder. Some vets ended up poor and homeless, and finding it too painful to endure the stress committed suicide. Acute psychiatric disturbances could be easily triggered by events (flashbacks) that recaptured the original trauma—the sounds of helicopter rotors whirring and gunfire, and even smells.

Vietnam 1967

"If you know the enemy and know yourself, you need not fear the result of a hundred battles." So says the proverb from Sun Tzu, ancient spiritual mentor and author of *The Art of War*. But what if you are a nineteen or twenty-year old American who hardly knows himself or the enemy? He's been shipped ten thousand miles from home to the front lines of war in Vietnam. He's in the war zone and must fight to stay alive.

Where did Paul Gardner, new enlistee, only twenty-years old, fit into the big scheme of military objectives? Paul was one of 500,000 troops that had been deployed to fight in Vietnam. The average age of enlisted men deployed was twenty-two. A few of the men were seventeen or eighteen . Two-thirds of the men who served in Vietnam were volunteers. Compare that to two-thirds of the men who served in World War II were drafted. Between 1964 and 1973 volunteers outnumbered enlisted troops by nearly four to one. After enlisting in April and going through basic training at the US Army Aviation Center at Fort Rucker, Alabama, Paul was stationed at Camp Enari (Pleiku Air Base), in Pleiku, in the Central Highlands of Vietnam. Pleiku was strategically important during the Vietnam War because it was the primary terminus of the military supply logistics corridor extending westwards along Highway 19 from the coastal population center and port facilities of Qui Nhơ. At that point in time, 14,000 American soldiers had already died.

Military Occupational Specialty (MOS): Each of the MOS requires advanced individual training and specialization. Paul was a Spec-4. In the minds of most of the young recruits their call of duty was simply to kill the enemy. That played out in various deadly missions like search and destroy, rescue, and bombardment, and an operation to interrupt and halt movement of enemy troops and supplies along the Ho Chi Minh Trail. This continued until November 1968.

Tactically, the war in Vietnam was not a ground war. It was a helicopter war. Fundamentally, the war was one in which the speed of the deployment of men and support from firepower was absolutely vital. The firepower came from the Huey gunship helicopter that had become a crucial element in the logistical support of thousands of troops that were being deployed. The Bell UH-1 Iroquois (nicknamed the "Huey") is a turbine-powered military helicopter. The Huey's lethal power as an attacking air combat gunship led to its quick rise from workhorse to legend Army UH-1's totaled 9,713,762 flight hours in Vietnam between October 1966 and the end of American involvement in early 1973. Paul was assigned as a door gunner on the Huey in 1967. Paul's memoir follows his enlistment and deployment in Vietnam to his war zone experience as helicopter gunner aboard the Huey gunship.

Chapter 1

DON'T TELL MOM

As we left the South China Sea behind us and the country of South Vietnam came in to view, the pilot came on the loud speaker and said: "Gentlemen, welcome to Vietnam!" *No explosions, no craters, no nothing. I guess that's good.*

≈≈≈

It's 1965, and I had just graduated from Rush-Henrietta Senior High School, Henrietta, New York, a suburb of Rochester. I was by no means a great student, but I showed up every day and enjoyed my years there. In my senior year I was accepted to a technical college in Toronto, Canada. But my guidance counselor told me he didn't think that school was for me. He thought I would make a good salesperson instead. I believed him and decided not to go to technical school. It was a decision that would set off a chain events that would change my life forever. My father often spoke of the school of hard knocks—the "University of Life." He said, "Oh, the Army will do you good. They'll make a man out of you." I was not very close to my father, but I would realize and admit to myself later in life that I did the things I did to prove to him that I was worthy of his praise. No matter that I would ever receive a pat on the back.

The Vietnam war was in the news more and more each day. I recall the Army's first major contact with the PAVN (People's Army of Vietnam) or NVA (North Vietnam Army) in a far-away place called Ia Drang Valley. Little did I know then that I'd encounter those enemy soldiers in less than two years. Escalation was in progress, and the draft was about to be the ruin of dreams for many young men. Eighteen-years old and a high school grad with no plans on going to college was a surefire way to end up in the military. The fact was that I never thought eighteen-year-olds should have a plan anyway. Party, cars and girls seemed like a good plan, so I went with it. I worked for a local bank for a few months, but I knew a decision on my future was coming, and the military seemed to be the answer. My first choice was the Navy. My father served in the Navy during WWII at Iwo Jima and Okinawa, so I guess that sounded most likely. Flying a helicopter gunship never crossed my mind. I'm not sure if I ever heard of one in 1965. Submarines sounded pretty exciting.

I went to Buffalo, New York, and took all sorts of tests, passed them all, and when I met with my recruiter and was informed the enlistment requirement was six years after a two-year wait, I balked. Eight years is a long time—too long. The Air Force required four years enlistment, another two-year wait. I never considered the Marines. One day I was walking by the Army recruiter, stuck my head in the door and said, "What do you have available that's exciting?" I felt like I was shopping for a new car. "How about helicopters?" the recruiter replied. "No waiting!"

I signed up in early February, took a physical in March and got my orders to report to Ft. Dix, New Jersey, for basic training. I arrived April 11, 1966. I actually liked basic training, and I was promoted to squad leader after three weeks and platoon leader when the current one got ill. I felt good about my decision to enlist and never regretted it. I owed my newly found confidence to a Staff Sergeant Flowers. He was a huge black man that was a legend at Ft. Dix. Sgt. Flowers was the best. I would give anything to thank him for pointing me in the direction I was destined to travel. He asked me why I enlisted. I didn't know for sure back then, but I think I wanted more control of my future. More than one family member and friend tried their best to change my mind but to no avail. I watched and read enough about what soldiers endured during war, so infantry was not for me. Bopping around the countryside in a helicopter seemed a lot safer.

Basic training was over. Ft. Rucker, Alabama, was the home of Army Aviation, and it's there I would learn my trade as a helicopter mechanic/crew chief. The training lasted a few months. While there we were given a test, and I scored high enough that I was offered the opportunity to either go to OCS (Officer Candidate School) or Warrant Officer Flight School at Ft. Wolters, Texas. I chose flight school, and after a couple weeks leave at home I was heading to Texas. Ft. Wolters was located west of Dallas/Ft. Worth at Mineral Wells, Texas. Flight school was grueling and classes were long. I had a hard time staying awake, especially during map reading.

After a few weeks I soloed on a Hiller H-55 and felt pretty good about myself. Map reading was difficult for me, and even though I didn't know it at the time, I realize now I had an attention deficit that I still have today. Two days after my solo flight, I went up with an instructor pilot. While making an auto-rotation, I suddenly had a severe headache—a migraine sort of pain. The instructor pilot took control of the H-55 and landed us, immediately grounded me and ordered me to the infirmary.

After a two-night hospital stay and a series of blood tests and examinations, I was released but remained grounded. I attended all of the other required classes, but I was not allowed to fly unattended. Then it happened. I was back in the barracks three days after my hospital release. I was arranging my locker, and while placing my dress shoes on top of my locker, I suddenly became very faint and collapsed on the floor. I came to shortly after as medics stood over me shining a tiny flashlight in my eyes. I spent that night in a hospital bed, and upon my release I was ordered to the commanding officer's office. After a little conversation, I was washed out of the flight program with a medical elimination. Disappointed at first, I was later relieved. The thought of having the responsibility for the safety of others apparently was more than I could handle. Disappointed, yes, but surrender, no. There was a place for me. I just needed to find it.

I would spend the next couple of weeks waiting for reassignment by driving a bus that would ferry troops to and from the airfield. Three days a week I would drive a certain route delivering officers to their offices. On or about my twentieth birthday, I received my orders. Korea? No way. My buddies Lee Heidenfelt and John Galarno were there. They had written me and told me to go anyplace but Korea. It was cold, dreary, had poor accommodations and the food sucked. On my officer delivery route my last stop was the office of a Colonel. I struck up a conversation with him and discovered he was the "man" who reassigned soldiers to their next duty. I explained that Korea was not an option for me and requested an interview. He said to come see him at 0900 hours tomorrow and he'd see what's available. I was at the Colonel's office before he was. His secretary, a PFC from Someplace, New Jersey, got me a coffee and told me the Colonel would be here soon.

The Colonel looked larger than I remembered as he entered the Army green painted building. He looked at me and struggled to remember why I was here. "Sir, I met you on the bus. I'm the guy who doesn't want to go to Korea." He settled in to his cushy chair and pulled out a notepad. Shortly after getting my serial number and a little casual conversation, he sat upright, leaned back in his chair, looked directly at me and said, "Why on earth would you do that?" Somewhat startled by his question, I took a few seconds to respond. "Sir, my ancestors were in the American Revolution, War of 1812, Civil War, WWI and II, and the Korean War. I can't be the only generation that didn't do his part. He paused and then sifted through a folder and asked once more, "Are you sure, son?" Moments of silence suddenly ceased when he said, "I can send you to the Central Highlands in Vietnam with the 4th Division." I hope with an aviation unit, sir," I said. "Yes," he said. "Consider it done then." He stood up, walked around the desk and shook my hand.

"Don't tell your mother, son."

"I won't, sir. Thank you." He called his PFC Secretary in, handed him the necessary information from the aforementioned folder and instructed him to get the necessary forms prepared in order for him to sign. I was to return two days later and hand carry those orders back to my company commander. The lifetime experience that you can't buy, rent, borrow or watch on a reality show was about to unfold for this just turned twenty-year-old "boy." Mom never found out!

On my short leave before my long journey to Southeast Asia, I spent a lot of time with friends at local bars. I often felt I was seeing them for the last time the way they treated me. It's June 1967 and the Vietnam conflict is escalating. U.S. troop deployment was approaching 500,000, and by 1968 it would reach 536,000. I never thought for a moment I was making a mistake. I heard of a few high school classmates that chose to go to Canada to avoid the draft. I was asked by another friend how I felt about that. *Life is about choices,* I reckoned. Every day of our lives we make choices. I made mine; they made theirs. I harbor no ill feelings against them and I have carried that attitude with me my whole life.

My last few days were spent with family. My grandparents were the ones I cared for the most. They were always supportive, and they would be the last ones I would disappoint. My last Saturday night at home was spent with family at the local Cartwright Inn, enjoying a great meal with Mom, Dad, two brothers and four sisters. The owners of the inn would lose their twenty-four-year-old son, Lt. Thomas Cartwright. Lt. Cartwright would be shot down and killed in late June 1967 only days after my last supper before shipping out. I didn't quite know that kind of pain yet, but as time went on I would, and I would feel it for others, others I didn't even know.

Mom, Dad, brothers and sisters took me to Rochester Airport. A strange occurrence took place there. As I said my good-byes to my family, my father, with tears in his eyes, hugged me and told me to be careful and come home safely. I boarded the plane, spotted an available window seat and I took it. I looked out at where I exited the airport for the plane, and standing there was my entire family framed in the big plate window. I knew right then and there I'd be home to see that very sight again, my family in reverse of today. I never had a doubt. Somehow I knew that scene would be recreated.

Oakland, California was my final destination today. On arrival we (three other GI's I met at the baggage terminal) were bussed a short distance to our home for a day or two. We were given bunks in a huge warehouse. Then we went through a medical barrage of shots, pills and warnings about disease, poor water quality and sexually transmitted diseases. We stayed in the bunk-bed warehouse for three nights. The next night a soldier (I have a picture but no name) from back East scored two tickets for a concert in San Francisco. I was surprised they would let us leave the barracks, but they did. We saw a relatively new group called Jefferson Airplane. We couldn't have been more out of place. The entire crowd had long hair, beads, tie-dyed clothes and reeked of marijuana.

The following day was the same as the day before—a lot of sitting around. Evening mess was lousy. When we got back to our area, our orders were clear. Breakfast at 0400 hours, 0600 board a bus for Oakland, 0700 board aircraft, next stop Pleiku, Vietnam. A few of guys were in a panic. Some Sergeant came around and warned us that anyone caught with alcohol on the flight would get an Article 15. Actually, the punishment was basically a wrist slap and a fine. I went to the latrine, and I couldn't believe all these guys dumping the bottles of alcohol in the trash can. I grabbed three bottles, tucked them away in my bag.

Our flight over was to be on a huge Air Force jet. We got to the loading area, but there was no jet to be seen. Well, things don't always go as planned in the Army. We waited in a hangar for hours for the aircraft to arrive. We occupied ourselves with playing catch with anything that looked like a ball or frisbee. I remember looking around the hangar at all these young boys who would soon be men and thinking, *Do any of us know what we are in for, or are we just young, naïve and stupid?*

We finally boarded the huge Air Force jet. This plane was big, really big. The seats weren't the best, but we could get up and move around. About eight or nine hours into the flight, we were informed that a mechanical malfunction had occurred and that we would be landing at Wake Island for repairs. We deplaned and were told to take our personal belongings and walk down the ramp to the waiting area. We had been there about an hour when we were told to make ourselves comfortable. Our "Vietnam taxi" would be ready to go in six hours. "Six hours?" the guys cried out. Ooh man, I sure wish I had that bottle I threw in the trashcan back in Oakland.

There were three or four guys I hung with. I suggested we go sit on the beach and wait this out. I opened my bag, showed them the three shiny bottles of gin, vodka and bourbon. "Holy shit, I'll get the cups," one of the guys said. On this beautiful moonlit night we sat at the Wake Island Memorial on a perfect Pacific Ocean evening and commenced to getting hammered. I have no idea what time it was but we got called back to the aircraft. All I remember is that it was dark. With a little help from my friends, I was able to get back on the aircraft. I can only assume we took off and proceeded to our final destination, because the next thing I know we are landing at Camp Holloway, Pleiku, Vietnam. On the final approach everyone was trying to look out a window to see what this place we all had heard about was like. Was it burning with huge holes in the ground, explosions going off, little yellow men running all over the place? No, none of that. We grouped in a formation and waited for your name to be called. Once called, they pointed you to a troop truck and ten of us were sent to Camp Enari.

After a two-day orientation, I was separated from these guys and sent to DIVARTY Aviation. I was welcomed by a Specialist 5 John McConnell, given a tour, a bunk, an introduction to those who lived in this hooch and told to report to the airfield operations tent at 0600. Thus my Vietnam experience had begun. It was July 1967.

Chapter 2

THE VILLAGE

At night when the moonlight doesn't interfere with darkness, the stars seem to be right on top of you. Three 122 mm enemy rockets went screaming overhead tonight with a trail of sparks and smoke visible as they burned propellant on the way to their target, giving "the rocket's red glare, the bombs bursting in mid-air" a new meaning.

≈≈≈

August 1967

I have been assigned to Camp Enari, home of the 4th Infantry Division near Pleiku, in the Central Highlands, Republic of South Vietnam ("The Nam"). Getting to know my brother crew chiefs and pilots won't take long, but I do feel somewhat distant from some of them, as we all come from different walks of life and parts of the country. We vary in education, intelligence, and ethnic background. One thing we all had in common, however, was that we were young men. No, we were boys. Most of us were away from home for the first time in our lives, and it was our first war, though for some it would be our last!

I'm starting to wonder if there is actually a war in progress. I've witnessed a lot of aircraft coming and going, but with the exception of a distant explosion I saw no evidence of a military conflict, especially like the one I read about in the papers and seen on the nightly news. The weather was OK—60-70 degrees and cool at night and somewhat dreary. I was told by a short-timer that May through October is monsoon season and the cold and damp would be over soon. I had yet to leave Camp Enari for any reason, but that was about to change. I had not been assigned an aircraft yet, so I was looking for a reason to get out there and see what I was missing.

Its mid-August. At the daily morning formation Capt. Asbury, Company Commander, announced that they needed volunteers for a Civil Affairs team. I looked at a corporal standing next to me, and with my puzzled look he gathered that I had no idea what a Civil Affairs team was, did, or was supposed to do.

The corporal gave me the abbreviated definition. The CA Team would visit villages and provide medical aid to those in need. "How long are they gone? I asked.

"About two or three days," he replied. "I had been on a couple of them, and it was pretty safe for the most part."

"Sounds good enough to me," I said.

I approached a Lieutenant that I had seen once before and offered my services. He said that I was to report here tomorrow morning at 0600. He gave me a list of essential equipment I would need. I saluted him and guaranteed my attendance.

I hardly slept that night, and before I attempted slumber I was tortured by my hooch mates. Volunteer for nothing they teased. I found myself volunteering for convoys and other adventures over the next few months as an escape from the base camp doldrums. My eagerness to be involved, however, would have its drawbacks one day.

We loaded on trucks in the morning and we were on our way. A firebase/outpost called the Oasis was our destination where we would connect with an armored unit, a medical team and others. I recall that there were about twelve of us plus the two APC (Armored Personal Carrier) crews, radio operators and two officers. The medics carried sidearms and had Red Cross patches on their helmets and shirts.

APC's are not exactly luxury cars and they provide no comfort whatsoever. With no chance of looking out a window (they have no windows) and having no clue where we were or where we were going, I quickly second-guessed my decision to make this adventure my first one. Suddenly, the APC came to an abrupt halt. Once the rear ramp opened, I rejoiced at the daylight and freedom from the horror of a bunch of boys and their pungent body odors. They lined us up in a military formation, gave us a bunch of do's and don'ts, and on foot we single-filed down a narrow path to a destination that would soon reveal itself.

About an hour into our march the Lieutenant that I had met the night before now had a name—Lt. Glen McWilliams from Buffalo, New York. "Hey, I'm from that area!" I exclaimed. We connected immediately and shared our experiences, landmarks and hangouts in the Buffalo area. Shortly after Lt. McWilliams and I discovered each other, the march came to a halt and he told us to take ten. "Smoke 'em if you got 'em!" he said. Almost everyone smoked cigarettes, and at a dollar a carton you couldn't afford not to smoke. Lt. McWilliams pulled me aside and presented me with an offer: "I would like you to move to the point."

"The point?" I asked.

"Yeah, we are getting close to the village, and I want you to lead us in and experience what I saw a few weeks ago. You will someday look back on these upcoming moments as life changing events."

I had no idea what to expect from the invitation that had been bestowed upon me. All sorts of thoughts raced through my mind as we weaved up the narrow trail leading to this alleged life changing event. While I fought off flying insects, vines and other obstructions, I glanced back at Lt. McWilliams, hoping he would give me a clue. I realized that wasn't probably going to happen, so I cautiously made my way down the trail.

This was my first off-base camp event since I arrived almost six weeks ago. My M16 rifle was locked and loaded, but I'm not sure if I could react or know how to react if danger presented. Walking directly behind me was a seasoned infantry soldier who had that 'oh so obvious' drawl that quickly identified him as a Southern boy. I felt he was my security blanket if I needed one.

11

The trail took a turn, and the smell of burning wood was now present thus signaling we were getting close to a village. When I came to a fork in the trail, I stopped and looked at Lt. McWilliams for direction. With a hand motion he instructed me to take the left turn. As I ducked under a low hanging tree limb and rose back to an upright stance, I saw the thatched roofs of a village a mere one hundred yards in front of me. Lt. McWilliams nodded, signaling that we had reached our destination.

My once steady gait was interrupted when my eyes locked on an elderly man raising his hand in a welcoming gesture. I returned the smile until I noticed his hand was absent fingers. As I drew nearer it became apparent that not only his absent fingers but his nose was eaten away. His ears were nubs, and part of his jaw revealed more of his teeth than you would normally see. Lt. McWilliams quickly moved ahead of me and the Southern drawling infantryman. Close behind us were the medics. I stood motionless and oblivious to anything else as a group of villagers approached us. Oh my God, all of these people had hideous deformities—children and adults. Some were legless, armless. Some crawled, hobbled and managed to come closer with their make-shift crutches to the awaiting medical team.

Three things became very clear. First, Civil Affair teams had been here before. Secondly, I'm in the middle of a nightmare. Thirdly, I am smack in the middle of a leper colony. As my eyes darted from one poor soul to another, I remembered reading about these colonies in the Bible. I thought, *Wait a minute! This is 1967. How could this be?* Now standing next to me was another rookie soldier who was going through a similar horrifying revelation. I don't recall his name or where he was from, but I could have cared less at that juncture of my life, especially what I was going through emotionally. I looked at him and he looked at me, and without a single word being said we were able to sense each other's utter shock and growing sadness of what we were witnessing.

The rookie and I shared a common task: to observe the surrounding area for possible VC. I wondered, *Hell, what does a VC even look like?* They wouldn't really trust us two twenty-year-old kids to protect them, would they? The rookie and I were running low on C-rations after a few children had begged them away from us. The sad, dark, hopeless eyes of a severely handicapped and disfigured boy made eye contact with me. My heart sank as he approached. Other than my M16, I would have given this unfortunate soul anything. His somewhat deformed hand reached out to me. All he wanted was to hold my hand.

Tears welled up in my eyes. I was paralyzed with sadness and felt compelled to do more. I handed the rookie my M16, bent down and picked up the boy and held him close. He had to have felt my racing, pulsing heart. Lt. McWilliams approached me with a sadness in his voice and instructed me to put the boy down, which I did immediately.

"I have another job for you," said the Lieutenant. "Come with me." As I walked away I turned slowly and looked at the boy once more. He was enjoying my last C-ration. Army C-rations were not something you actually enjoyed. In truth, the dates on most of the C-Rats were WWII vintage or earlier.

We walked to the other side of the village, which appeared to be somewhat larger than I thought. We weaved in and out passing by grass hut after grass hut. Some had corrugated metal which was likely scrounged from somewhere and was now serving as building material. One roof had a Coca Cola sign, another a colorful metal sign expounding on the rich flavor of a beer called Tiger 33.

At the end of the village was another team of GI's. I wondered, *Where did these guys come from?* I didn't recognize any of them. They hadn't come with us. I found out later it was an interrogation team from a Special Forces unit. They even dressed differently with their camouflage fatigues, special weapons and soft, brimmed hats. Some had berets and one of them had an Australian accent. Make no mistake: each one of them took their duties seriously.

These guys—enlisted men—had more stripes of rank than our group combined.

As I got closer, I discovered there was a young Vietnamese male being interrogated. He could have been not more than fourteen–years-old, but they all seemed younger to me. The young man was reluctant to answer any questions, which by the way were being asked in Vietnamese.

The soldier leading the way with the questions was getting irritated by the lack of progress. He looked over at an SP4 (Specialist 4) with a crank-phone in his hand and said, "Encourage our young friend." The Spec. 4 gave the crank phone about ten good turns, and to the horror of my first day in the bush I realized the electricity generated was being transferred through two wires to a couple of moistened metal rings on the young man's wrists.

It didn't take a brain surgeon to figure out the young man was a suspected VC. He screamed in agony as the Spec.4 cranked the handle. The jolts of electricity stood his hair on end and a wet spot emerged near his genital area. I had to turn away as this didn't seem right that we would resort to this type of interrogation method. I would find out over time that this was common practice.

A short distance away I saw three other suspected VC's awaiting their turn on the crank-phone. They stood the first suspect up, bound his hands and feet and dragged him to a spot around the corner so as to be out of sight from the others. Lt. McWilliams motioned me to follow him and I did. He said, "If your gun is not locked and loaded, do it now. If he runs, shoot him." So, it turned out that my first and only Civil Affairs job was to guard the suspected VC and kill him if necessary. When I was fourteen, I was grounded for shooting a robin with my pellet gun. I wondered, *What would Mom say if she knew this?* As I stood behind him, I couldn't help but see the burn marks on his wrist and a look of total despair and fear flooding his face.

In a matter of minutes my emotions soared off the charts. I experienced many troubling emotions in just a short period of time. I continued to guard my suspected VC. I think the watch lasted for about forty-five minutes to an hour. He looked at me often, and I would look the other way. I thought I can't imagine the fear he was experiencing or what was in store for him.

I was relieved of my guard duty shortly thereafter, as Lt. McWilliams announced we were heading back to the APC's to spend the night. As we left the village I figured there were about two hours of daylight remaining. I'd grown accustomed to the village smell and didn't pay much attention to it as we walked away. I looked back several times at the people, the village and the "event." Today in retrospect, I remember it just like I saw it that day.

I never did see the interrogation team leave the village. They either left in a different direction or they were still there. No telling what they were doing. We took a different trail back, and I learned later you never take the same trail back to avoid an enemy ambush. *Good thinking*, I thought. We descended down a hill, and low and behold, a beautiful Montagnard village was lying ahead of us. As we entered, I couldn't believe how neat and clean it was. A crystal-clear stream was to our right and to our left a grove of banana trees—tiny bananas about half the size of your typical banana. Lt. McWilliams instructed us not to touch them unless offered by one of the villagers. Montagnards (or Dega as they call themselves) are a tribal people of the Malayo-Polynesian and Mon Khmer language groups, some thirty tribes of which live in the central highlands of Vietnam. The villagers are small in stature but big in smiles and kindness. It is estimated that over 200,000 Montagnards died and 85 percent of their villages were destroyed during the Vietnam war. They were a loyal ally of our military and deserved much better than that. A group of friendly villagers approached us and offered us bananas and rice wine. We had pretty much run out of C-Rations, having given most of them away at the leper village. In return for their gifts, we gave them matches, lighters and cigarettes and what few goodies we had remaining. On leaving, almost everyone looked back as if to take a mental photograph

15

of this quaint little village. Two villages, two totally different memories.

One good thing about Vietnam: the absence of light pollution provided a darkness that unveiled billions of stars and constellations in the sky. As I stared out at the universe above me, I finished my special banana and fell asleep with the day's events behind me. The little kid's face from the leper colony was probably my last thought that ran through my mind before I fell asleep.

I have been heavily involved in charitable foundations that revolve around children for over forty years. Currently, I'm on the board of the HUGS Foundation here in Rochester, New York. It's a foundation that treats children with various birth defects. We go to South America and, you guessed it, Vietnam. Go figure.

Chapter 3

BE CAREFUL WHAT YOU ASK FOR!

A disturbing fact of the Vietnam war was the kill ratio established by Secretary of Defense Robert McNamara, President Lyndon Johnson and others in the administration. That ratio was believed to be 10:1. In other words, our leaders decided that it was OK for soldiers to keep dying as long as 10 North Vietnamese soldiers died for each American. Let that sink in! Please note that no president, senator, congressman or general would volunteer themselves or anyone they cared for to be part of that horrific ratio.

≈≈≈

September turned to October and I was still waiting for my own aircraft. I had to wait for someone to go home for an aircraft to become available. SP5 O'Connell from someplace in the Midwest was nearing the end of his twelve-month tour of duty. It looks like I may have my own OH-23.

SP5 John McConnell was heading home for good and he couldn't be happier. He told me I was getting his aircraft. "It's about friggin' time!" I shouted. He was also our section leader and would dish out duties each day. He seemed to appreciate my eagerness to help him, and in trade he would keep me off KP (Kitchen Police). You had to report to the kitchen at 0530 and you were done when they said so.

I loved convoys, and I would drive the five-ton trucks that were filled with supplies to firebases like the Oasis, Jackson Hole, and others. Not once did we have an ambush or sniper take a shot at us. The big day arrived. SP5 O'Connell was going home and was packed and ready to go. Goodbye hugs and you "lucky bastard" comments came from every direction. McConnell was oblivious to our goodbyes as he loaded his duffel bag on the Jeep for his ride to Pleiku and home.

Maj. Z was our commanding officer by rank, but Capt. Bacon seemed to be the lead officer. We were told as we said our goodbyes that there would be a section formation in the morning to distribute new duties now that McConnell was gone. I would find out what 23 would be mine. I was sure to be a shoe in. About 0800 hours Maj. Z, Capt. Bacon, and Lt. Rich walked in together. We gathered in our little hooch, and they announced that Rich Perona would be getting O'Connell's aircraft. I was floored and the look of disappointment on my face must have been obvious because Capt. Bacon immediately announced that I was now the section leader.

"We asked Specialist McConnell who was best candidate to become the new section leader," Capt. Bacon said. He looked at me and said, "You were the guy, and so as of this moment you are in charge of all seven aircraft and the crew chiefs assigned to them."

I didn't quite know how to react. I was stunned, disappointed and flattered that they thought that much of me. I only wanted one aircraft. I now have seven. I guess that's better.

Being a section leader had its privileges. No KP! It was my responsibility to assure the pilots that all aircraft were in proper running order and each crew chief performed all service and safety inspection before each flight. The Company 1st Sergeant would require a daily list of those available for details: Civil Affairs Teams, truck drivers for provision transport to outlying firebases, guard duty, and other often menial tasks. I had a five-ton truck driver's license, and on a few occasions I sent myself. It was a great escape from the daily boredom that still was a real problem for me.

By October my desire to be more involved was starting to wear me out. Every day I asked the pilots if they would mind if I could accompany them. Some did, some didn't. The fall months in the Pleiku area were very quiet as far as "wars" go, so the pilots were limited on missions and often became pressed into taxi service for higher ranking officers.

This period of quiet and lack of enemy activity was about to change as October came to an end. Helicopter gunships from the 17th Air Cav and 4th Aviation B Company were making numerous runs day and night as NVA and VC Units were making noise in the nearby provinces.

I had made friends with David Iverson, a crew chief from B Company's Gambler Guns over the past months, and I often voiced my desire to become a door gunner on one of these awesome machines.

Late in the day on November 3, 1967, the lives of four families and scores of friends and relatives would be changed forever when they were to learn that the four young men they saw off to this far away land would not be coming home. B Company's Gambler Gun, UH-1C 66-00538 was lost, and the two pilots—one crew chief/door gunner and one door gunner—were gone forever. Nonetheless, they do live within a brotherhood that I will attempt to explain later.

In Memory

1st Lt. James E. Pavlicek, Jr. Panel 29E Line 17

WO 1 David E. Thomas. Panel 29E Line 17

SP4 James E. Anderson. Panel 29E Line 13

SP4 Randall W. Ernsberger. Panel 29E Line 13

David Iverson, the B Company crew chief, who I had gotten to know, stopped by our hooch on November 4th. Grieving over the loss of an entire crew, David mentioned that he had often flown with SP 4 Randall Ernsberger. The pain on David's face was unmistakable.

David explained that there were no replacements readily available for the lost crew. He asked me if I could get permission from my CO

19

(Company Commander) and would present my desire to volunteer to fill the vacancy. I immediately went to Capt. Bacon and told him of the vacancy at 4th Aviation.

"I'm not surprised," Capt. Bacon said. "If you're sure this is what you want, then I will approve the transfer." After a brief pause I said, " I believe it is, sir." I never once imagined I would have this opportunity because of somebody dying.

"David assured me that we have a great bunch of guys. I've told them about you, and you'll be fine."

I asked Capt. Bacon, "I think I should go sleep on this. Can I decide tomorrow?"

"Of course," Capt. Bacon said.

I never doubted for a moment that I wanted this. The very next day I reported to 4th Aviation. It was November 5, 1967. My reporting to this gunship unit was about to set in motion a series of events unlike those of the previous months. To say that I was excited about the prospects of flying on a gunship would be a huge understatement.

I first had to meet with the 4th Aviation's commanding officer, Maj. Gordon, to assure him of my desire to join B Company. It would be Maj. Gordon's stamp of approval that was necessary for this transfer. I really didn't know how to approach this "job interview."

He got right to the point: "Why do you want this? You do realize that the life expectancy of helicopter crews in combat is pretty low?"

"I need to be more involved, sir," I answered.

"Capt. Bacon gave you a great recommendation, but you have no actual combat experience, or for that matter other than a few convoys you haven't been off base much." I didn't know how to respond to these questions, but finally I said, "Sir, I need more than what I've done the last few months. Maj. Gordon, you need a gunner and I want to be that soldier. I can do this, sir."

20

Maj. Gordon paused for what seemed like minutes. "Go back to your unit," the Major replied. Dead silence took over the room. I got the feeling that I was not what he was looking for. I stood up, saluted him and thanked him for his time and made my way to the door. As my hand touched the door handle, Maj. Gordon spoke once more. "While you're there, pick up your belongings and report to 1st Sgt. Barry. He'll get you set up with a bunk and show you around." Maj. Gordon finished by saying, "You do understand that this is a ninety-day temporary assignment?" I was speechless.

Then Maj. Gordon said, "Welcome aboard, trooper."

"Thank you, sir," I said with more than a touch of relief and excitement.

I walked as fast as I could back to my hooch, said goodbye to the guys, took about an hour to pack and was on my way to meet 1st Sgt. Barry.

First Sgt. Barry was as likable as a Sergeant could be. He was pushing twenty years of service, a little chubby, half bald, spoke with a Jersey accent, but he seemed the type that if you'd respect his rank, you'll do just fine. "Follow me," he said. We hadn't walked too far when he stopped at a relatively new barracks, opened the door, motioned me to enter and wished me luck.

There was hardly anyone in the barracks when I arrived. A young blonde-haired soldier at the end of the row of bunks asked me if I needed help. First Sgt Barry introduced me to Gary Diescher from Alton, Illinois. "Specialist Diescher will find you a place to sleep and where to put your gear," said 1st Sgt. Barry as he turned and left the hooch. Gary pointed to an available bunk, showed me which locker was mine and then went about his detail of sweeping the floor.

While filling the locker with my stuff, I couldn't help but notice that the name on the locker was only partially removed. It didn't take Dick Tracy to surmise that this locker was that of Randall Ernsberger. My new locker and bunk were occupied only a few days ago by the late door gunner. I stood there looking at the locker, at the poor job of removing his name and thinking about the alleged mortality rate of door gunners. Nineteen-year-old SP-4 Randall Wayne Ernsberger had arrived in country three weeks after me, and he is now on his way to Phoenix, Arizona to a grieving family awaiting the remains of their boy. I'm glad we never met. Randall is buried at Sugar Grove Cemetery in Elkhart County, Indiana.

The one thing I remember most about that day was the music. One of the crew chiefs had a SONY reel-to-reel tape player that played "Sgt. Pepper's Lonely Hearts Club Band" twenty-four hours a day. I mean twenty-four hours a day--every hour, every minute of the day. "Lucy in the Sky with Diamonds" was on when I entered my new home. Flashback? Oh yeah! Music played a big role with us there. Whether it was rock 'n roll, classical or country, it was music that relieved the tensions of the day and the events that filled them.

I spent the next day getting a briefing on the way they did things. I was issued an armor vest, an M60 and a flight helmet. My friend, Dave, took me to the gunship to which I was assigned. It was a Frog. A Frog is a UH 1B that was outfitted differently than most other gunships. The Frog had twice as many rockets, a nose-mounted 40 mm cannon and two door gunners with bungee corded M60 machine guns.

We were on our way back to the barracks when our pilots (who will remain nameless as I have forgotten their names) were running to the airfield. Dave looked at me and said, "Let's go." We ran to the flight HQ, grabbed our helmets, M60s, ammo box and armor vest and hurried to our aircraft that was warming up. I would venture a guess that those articles weighed a hundred pounds or more. I hung my M60 on the bungee cord, placed the 1000 plus rounds of ammo onboard and proceeded to put my armor plates on. Dave shouted above the whine of the turbine motors to put only my front ceramic plate on. He saw my confused look and responded, "We sit on the back plate unless you want your balls shot off." This "scramble" to the gunship would be repeated many times in the next few months.

I connected my monkey strap securely around my waist as we hovered and slowly made our way to the runway. Dave explained in my earlier orientation that the monkey strap would keep me from falling out if I was shot or got careless. The soon to never-be-forgotten sound of those Lycoming T53-L-5 engines producing 960 shaft horsepower whining as they build power was chilling and never to be forgotten. The pilot increased throttle, and with the nose tilted forward the UH 1B slowly gained altitude, and I was now officially on my first combat mission on a helicopter gunship in the Republic of South Vietnam. Far removed from 17 Valiant Drive in Henrietta, New York, I was about to get what I asked for.

Duc Co (pronounced Due Ko) was our destination. A LRRP (Long Range Recon Patrol) was in trouble and in danger of being wiped out. There was no time to spare. The air got chilly as we gained altitude and sped south to Duc Co. We flew for about twenty minutes as the adrenaline rush took over my internal clock mechanism. Radio chatter between our pilots and others on the ground sounded like a foreign language to me. I couldn't understand the slang and jargon of those soldiers on the ground as they gave directions to our pilots on where to focus their rockets and mini-guns. I had no idea what to do. *Where do I shoot?* I wondered. I was too embarrassed to ask, so I reckoned whatever Dave does, I do.

Darkness was setting in as I leaned forward to see what I could see. All of a sudden with no warning the pilot touched off half of the rockets from the very pod only inches away from where I sat. The noise and flames from the rocket pod and Dave's M60 startled me. I about jumped out of my skin, and then all of a sudden they released more rockets making their way to a target that I knew nothing about. I leaned out and forward and continued firing my M60 at the area that the rockets were heading. The pilot banked a hard left, keyed his microphone and said we were making one more run. Having never done this before, I waited to see what direction the pilots were sending those 2.75 rockets before I pulled the trigger. We emptied everything—every rocket, every 40 mm grenade and all of the M60 that Dave and I had in our boxes. As I looked at the bottom of my now empty ammo box, there was a hand-written note that said, *If you are reading this, then a good day was had by all.*

The twenty-minute flight back to Camp Enari seemed short as I kept going over and over in my mind my first combat mission on 4th Aviation B Company UH-1B Gambler Guns gunship. By now my adrenaline tank was empty.

My first combat mission on a helicopter gunship was now history. The LRRP's had been extracted to safety, and I knew a little more than I did a few short hours ago. As I look back on that day and its events, I realize how many young men likely felt the same confusion and uncertainty that I did.

"Nice work," the pilot said. Little did he know I had no idea what I was doing.

"Thank you," I replied. You would have thought I had just discovered the cure for cancer when everyone in the barracks shouted out, "Congratulations," "good job," and "How'd it feel to break your cherry?" I never told them I came pretty close to filling my britches when those rockets exited the pods.

There were reports of NVA Regulars infiltrating the Dak To area. In fact, I eventually learned that most rumors were just that—rumors. More important was that the action I so wished for was about to come to fruition. Stories of NVA buildup in the Kon Tum Province were not exaggerated. Reports that NVA's 24th, 32nd, 66th and 174th regiments, totaling 7,000 well-trained, devoted to their cause young men just like us, were coming to town to kill us. These young men, constituting the NVA 1st Infantry Division had infiltrated the Dak To area and their goal was simple: destroy our Dak To and Ben Het firebases, which, in turn, would take pressure off their main supply road to the south, known infamously as the Ho Chi Minh Trail.

The well-known 173rd Airborne's "Sky Soldiers" were under the command of the 4th Division and were dispatched to the area along with Infantry units of the 1st of 8th Infantry, 1st Cavalry Division, the

335 AHC (Attack Helicopter Company) and more. (Go to https://www.4thinfantry.org/ for a better accounting of those units involved.)

The next few weeks would set the tone for the next five months of my duty in Vietnam.

The stage was being set for what we know now was a 33-day battle that would devastate the NVA Regulars and end the young lives of 376 American boys and damage another 1440.

First Sgt. Barry entered the barracks about 1900 hours and advised us that at 0500 hours we were to be ready to fly. Richie from Albany, New York spoke up and asked First Sgt. Barry where we were going. The Sergeant's lack of a reply had Dak To written all over it. Tomorrow, 0500 hours would get here quick enough.

Chapter 4

GREEN TRACERS

We are not about to send American boys nine or ten thousand miles away from home to do what Asian boys ought to be doing for themselves. —President Lyndon Johnson in a speech at Akron University on October 21, 1964, two weeks before the presidential election.

≈≈≈

It's November 8,1967. I didn't sleep much last night as I waited for 0500 hours to arrive. Most of us were at the operations hooch before the scheduled time. As we entered we couldn't help notice that all the pilots were already there. The enlisted men did not usually attend briefings. The briefing was simple. Be at Dak To runway at 0600. Be prepared, bring plenty of ammo and give 'em Hell. We were assigned to a newer C Model Huey that was outfitted with less rockets but sported two mini-guns. These mini-guns were amazing. Capable of firing 6,000 rounds a minute, they were electronically cycled to 2200 rounds to conserve ammo. Loading the ammo trays had to be done carefully so as not to jam the gun and be rendered useless. I had to observe and practice firing the mini-gun a few times before I could do it correctly by myself.

We hurried to our equipment lockers and made our way to the airfield. The adrenaline was flowing strong enough to make the weight of our armor vests, M60 and other equipment weightless. Not a word was spoken as we loaded our guns, rockets and the extra ammunition we were told to bring. The weather has been spectacular lately—blue skies and not a cloud in the sky as we lifted off. I felt a chill as I leaned out to look at Camp Enari slowly drifting out of sight. As we flew over Camp Holloway near Pleiku it became clear that this operation was a big one. Aircraft and long truck convoys were headed north. The

27

infamous Dak To lay ahead, and I could only imagine what we were in for.

It was only forty-five minutes or so since take off as Dak To came in to view. I was surprised how slow these Hueys were. It seemed like we should have been here sooner. The long airstrip was now visible and much longer than I had imagined. More impressive was the row of UH-1H troop transports and probably thirty UH-1C gunships lined up in a row preparing for something big . . . something really big. I felt a sense of importance that for at least this moment outweighed any fear.

Infantrymen from our own 4th Division and the "Sky Soldiers" of the 173rd Airborne were loading onto UH-1D Hueys at the far end of the airstrip. I noticed arm patches of the famous 1st Air Cavalrymen passing by us, weighed down with all the necessary equipment to do battle with the PAVN. (People's Army of Vietnam). This enemy—our adversary—was no pushover. These young men were from families just like us. They are young, brave, and invincible. This wasn't a game and this wasn't behind Mrs. Reed's garage. Thousands of these well-trained and capable soldiers are here in the Central Highlands with one thing in mind: kill Americans.

We hovered directly to the recently added fuel bladders and topped off our tanks. I struck up a conversation with a Sergeant from New Jersey. He commenced to tell me that this operation was already six or seven days old and that a lot of choppers had already been lost and the casualties were adding up fast. As we finished our re-fuel he wished us good luck. "I'll see you later," he said as he turned his attention to his next customer.

We hovered back to the airstrip, shut down and awaited our orders. The pilots were getting briefed by a distinguished looking Colonel and his staff. A makeshift command center with a large map on a large easel was visible to us as well as a junior officer and his wooden pointer depicting the focus of today's operation.

A door gunner from the 335th AHC (Attack Helicopter) approached us, bummed a smoke and shared with us that this was their fourth day on the operation. They had already lost three helicopters and a few crew members. One of those crew members killed was a good friend from his hometown in South Carolina. None of our guys had been involved in something this big, and we were all ears as he had our complete attention while he shared his stories of the ongoing battle and what we were in for. "Sit on your armor plate," he said through his cigarette smoke as he made his way back to his chopper.

Although the pilots had yet to return, my crewmate, Dave, and I checked and re-checked our equipment in total silence for takeoff and something we would carry with us forever. I kept thinking and reminding myself that this is what I wanted. My thoughts would often drift back to a family gathering or happy days with my grandparents on summer vacation in a family cottage in Canada. This seemed like a good time for those happy thoughts. Being around a bunch of twenty-year-olds who only a few months before were cruising in their cars at the local hotdog stand in Anytown, USA was a surreal thought that was probably not mine alone.

At least two hours had passed and we were in the same place. Cigarettes, coffee and plenty of conversation filled in the gaps of time between anticipation of upcoming engagement with the NVA and destiny. *Maybe they called it off*, Dave and I wondered. The pilots seemed anxious to get this show on the road and stood close by ready and willing.

There was no lack of activity around us. C-130's landed, unloaded supplies and troops. Air Force jets screamed above us heading south. 155 mm, 175 mm Long Toms and the 8-inch artillery pieces increased their rate of fire, and about that time we were ordered to prepare for takeoff. I could feel my heart beating faster, and a nervous fear and excitement took over me. A crew chief from another company said the artillery and F-4 Phantom jets were softening our targets and predicted we'd be in the mix of action soon enough.

Sometime around 1100 hours, pilots and crews started boarding their crafts, and it didn't take a rocket scientist to figure out we were about to engage the enemy somewhere south of Dak To. As we lifted off the metal revetment runway, I looked back from the right side where I manned my M60 and watched over twenty Army green Bell Helicopter UH-1B and C model gunships lift upward and follow us in a well-orchestrated procession toward an unknown hill. A few troops and gunships peeled off in another direction, making me think there were numerous engagements taking place at the same time. The pilot keyed up and said we were ten minutes from our target.

"If you have any questions, now is the time." I hesitated and then blurted out that I had only been on one assault mission before and wasn't sure what direction I should fire.

"Follow the rockets," said the pilot. "Better yet, aim at the green tracers." I looked at Dave and mouthed green tracers at the same time I was shrugging my shoulders. Dave and I were able to electronically talk to each other without including the pilots.

"The NVA have green tracers," David said. "Fire at where they are coming from." Never seen or heard of a green one. Ours were red.

The ten-minute flight to our target seemed a lot longer than that. As we drew near our target, the 335th's gunships moved to the right and front of us and began their assault midway up the hill. By now it's probably 1130 hours, and the sky is as blue as blue can be but not blue enough to hide the hundreds of green tracers that were streaming out of the trees below. I couldn't believe how many. *Fire flies,* I thought. Once our pilots saw where they were coming from, we banked hard right, and our column of gunships of six fire-breathing helicopters let go with a salvo of rockets, mini-guns and our M60s. It took no time at all, maybe two runs at our target, and all our mini-gun rounds and rockets were exhausted. I looked at my ammo box and I saw maybe twenty rounds left. Ahead of us, a gunship was limping back to Dak To. Flying slowly and obviously crippled by green tracers, our pilot keyed up and told that pilot that we would stay close until we knew they were safe.

The smoking, crippled gunship made a landing that you might expect from a bullet-riddled aircraft. Medics were waiting for it to land, and by the time we set down they extracted a seemingly lifeless door gunner onto a stretcher and began to frantically give him aid. Here was another reminder that this war was for real and that people—young people—die. Dave keyed up and said, "That was the gunship behind us that took all those hits. The look on Dave's face must have mirrored mine as we pondered the results of "the luck of the draw." *That could have been us,* I thought, and no doubt Dave was thinking the same.

With so many aircraft refueling and rearming at the same time, it took nearly an hour before we were ready to go again. A pilot from Buffalo, New York, was engaged in conversation with our pilots when an explosion at the far end of the runway interrupted his story. The NVA positioned on a hillside west of us launched a series of rockets and mortars at the runway and nearby fuel depot. Within a matter of a minute, an artillery group fired 155 cannons at the suspected site of the launch area and abruptly silencing the enemy barrage.

"Load up!" Warrant Officer Skinner shouted. The whining noise of over twenty Huey gunship turbine engines warming up is a sound only a few of us would recognize and remember. Our taxi down the runway and liftoff were without event, and as the nose of our gunship dipped down we gained enough speed to lift our heavily laden gunship. I looked back and watched a parade of gunships make their way to our next target unknown to both Dave and me. Gazing at the formation of gunships, I could only wonder, *Would all of us return to repeat this process all over again.*

As we approached our target, I couldn't tell if it was the same hill we assaulted earlier, but I did know the green tracers were the same. This hill seemed different as it appeared battered. Fires and smoke covered the mountain slopes. I spotted two burning helicopters, one of them marked with the Red Cross. It was a Huey Med-E-Vac, upside down and burning. I found out later the NVA would fire on the medevacs not while landing but on takeoff when loaded with wounded.

Our mini-guns and rockets sprang into action. I focused on their destination and quickly opened fire with my bungee-corded M60 in the direction of the target selected by our pilots. A flood of green tracers made it apparent that Charlie was still in business and had no intention of running away. Our first of two sorties on the hill expended one half of our ordnance. The barrel of my M60 was red hot from about 700 rounds of continuous fire. Red hot gun barrels are dangerous as they tend to "cook off" rounds without warning. I grabbed my asbestos glove and released the barrel and watched it fall into the triple canopy jungle below. I quickly put the fresh barrel on my M60 and prepared for another run. I don't recall how many rounds were in our wooden box, but the number 1,000 or more comes to mind. We banked hard to the right and took our position in a wagon wheel formation, preparing our ship for another gun-run on Hill 8 something. Green tracers, although not as many as before, seemed to be focused on us as we approached for what would be our last gun-run today. We emptied all of our rockets and mini-guns at the top of the hill. My ammo box was empty now and so was Dave's. As we turned this time to the left, the explicable sound of bullets passing through the floor overshadowed everything. Holes appeared like magic as we turned away from the smoldering hill. The pilots usually exhibited a certain calm that as a crew member you appreciate. This seemed different as they immediately keyed their intercoms to make sure we were OK. As I keyed my microphone to reply that I was OK, I felt a burning sensation on my lower back. I reached back not knowing what I was feeling when I suddenly felt a hot liquid. *Blood's not hot,* I thought. Our ship seemed to be struggling as I glanced at the pilots who seemed to be occupied more than usual. My mind was now in high gear, my back was burning, and the floor and ceiling were riddled with bullets.

A vibration accompanied by noises I'd never heard before signaled that we have a problem. I was at the mercy of two well-trained pilots and God. What's more, the burning on my back seemed to be spreading. I couldn't stand it anymore. I unbuckled and removed my shirt. It was a clear liquid. A bullet, no doubt a green tracer, had entered the aircraft and pierced a hydraulic line spewing hot hydraulic fluid on my back. *Better than blood,* I thought.

It was then that Dak To airfield came into sight. We were smoking some, but the pilots appeared to have it under control. As we got closer, I could see a burning aircraft that hadn't quite made it back, having stopped short of the runway. I could see the 1st Air Cav insignia on the nose. *Not one of ours,* I thought. I just hope those guys are OK. The vibration was now getting worse, and noises like parts not lubricated and rubbing together were becoming louder by the second. I made sure my seat belt was drawn tight, and so I braced for a rough landing. Ten feet off the ground we lost lift, and in a split second we dropped to the ground twenty feet or so short of the runway. The drop wasn't so bad, but that sudden stop was bone jarring.

I think it was about 1300 or 1400 hours, maybe later. Things happened so fast and with such intensity that what time it was didn't matter. We unbuckled and jumped off and ran away from our ride. Our gunship was done for the day or maybe forever. I looked at Dave as he removed his flight helmet and noticed blood dripping off his nose.

"Dave!" I yelled. "You OK?" He pulled his helmet off to reveal an inch-long gash from a bullet fragment that had found its way to Dave's forehead. We quickly moved away from our aircraft in case a fire started. The co-pilot, a young twenty-two-year-old boy from Maine, slowly climbed out of the ship. His blood-stained left leg was evidence of an enemy bullet that had passed through the floor and the meaty part of his calf. He claimed he never felt it until minutes before we landed. A fire crew was at the ready and feverishly looked for evidence of fire that never happened. Once we got the OK, we went about and surveyed the damage the green tracers had caused. I quickly found out where the warm liquid came from. A small hydraulic line had been severed and the hot hydraulic fluid was the culprit for my earlier discomfort. Dave went to the aid station to get patched up while

I collected our gear from the crippled gunship. We started counting bullet holes, and although all four of us came up with different numbers, we settled on twenty. This gunship was not fit to fly and would soon be hooked out by a CH 47 back to Camp Enari for repairs. As soon as an available aircraft was available, we would hitch a ride back to Camp Enari and either wait for our repaired ship to be operational or be assigned to another. I was relieved this day was over for us.

A few hours passed, and all we could do was watch as a coordinated flock of helicopters flew out, returned, reloaded, refueled and went out again. Radio chatter of distress calls and medevac distress calls flooded the airwaves. Medevac pilots were the most respected of all as they were the ones who would fly directly into harm's way usually under fire while landing or hovering for as long as it took to load wounded infantry men aboard and get them to safety. We witnessed one medevac that was loaded with wounded and that was shot down, losing their crew and the wounded infantry men. Not one of us spoke a word. We just looked the other way and went about our business. I learned that if you pretend it didn't happen, then maybe it didn't.

Our ride back to base camp arrived. We boarded with our stuff, and at least for today Dak To was history. We haven't seen the end of this place.

Chapter 5

THE NET

There are over 500,000 troops. That's a half a million American soldiers in Vietnam in late 1967. Every place we go it's nothing but trucks, jeeps, armored vehicles, artillery pieces and helicopters and airplanes of every size and configuration.

≈≈≈

I never got the "We gotta take that hill" deal! Dak To was all about hills and all about taking them—hills with no names, just numbers. The number was the elevation above sea level: Hill 724, 823, 882, 830, 1338 and the mother of all hills—875. Once gotten, soon forgotten.

We've spent two days doing nothing. We've cleaned our gear and readied ourselves for a replacement gunship. The intensity of battle at Dak To hasn't waned a bit. We will no doubt be going back there soon. The stories from our other gun crews and our neighbors—the 17th Air Cav—are pretty bad. Nobody has exact numbers, but ships were lost and the lives that flew them were gone too. The NVA don't give up. They are tenacious, brave, and dedicated to killing as many Americans as they can. Their numbers are strong and their will even stronger. I would often wonder how they got the strength and conviction to fight us knowing we had all this firepower: artillery, gunships, Air Force and Navy jets and especially the B-52's. The B-52's would shake the ground for miles around. I heard stories that even if the actual bomb didn't kill the NVA, the concussion of a 500 and 750 lb bomb would. Enemy soldiers were often found walking around aimlessly stunned and bleeding from their ears and mouths after such a strike.

It's November 11th. The Battle for Dak To is in full swing. There are fights for so many hills that we can't keep them straight. Where we are going, what hills or trails meant nothing to Dave and me, as we go where the pilots take us.

Dave and I were assigned to another gunship, as the one we were on the other day had not yet been repaired. We all enjoyed a day off. Every day was a Monday or Thursday or whatever you preferred, as they all seemed the same. First Sergeant Barry entered our mess tent while we were finishing our gourmet something or other. He called out the crew members that would be heading back to Dak To . . . at what else? Yes, 0600 hours. I was one of the lucky ones. The message from our section leader Sgt. Barry was "Be prepared."

We made our way back to our hooch to get ready. As we entered, there was a noticeable and somber mood looming, no music playing, no chatter, no nothing except an MP and a staff Sergeant emptying someone's locker. I whispered to Richie from Albany, New York, "What's up?" Richie answered, "One of the crew chiefs from an Air Cav unit was killed a few days ago, and they are sending his belongings home." I didn't know how to reply to Richie's comment, so I didn't respond.

I took the late Randall Ernsberger's locker only a short time ago, and now someone will be taking up residence in this guy's locker. I am amazed and somewhat disappointed on how we accept the loss of a brother. It's almost like we look the other way. It really didn't happen, no big deal, at least he's out of here! Strange! It was a phenomenon shared by all.

The word came down from our flight commander: departure for Dak To would indeed take place at 0600 hours. Some of the crew members could sleep through the anticipation of the next day's mission, but I was not one of them. I tossed and turned all night long. I got up a couple of times and stepped outside the hooch, lit up a smoke and engaged in star gazing. The sky was loaded with stars, and on this particular evening they seemed to be at arm's reach. Shooting stars were very visible since the sky without the moon was as black as you could ever imagine. Jerry Frimmel from Seattle joined me a few minutes later, and before long seven or eight of us stood out there looking at the universe. Tomorrow would be just another day in the life of a gunship crew flying into green tracers and whatever else they had to throw at us, but right now we were a fraternity of young men— "old boys"—and soldiers thinking of home and what it would be like to be there. Almost without exception I think of that night when I look to the stars.

≈≈≈

It's a beautiful day. The sun's up, no clouds, and it should be another perfect weather day. Great weather is an advantage to our side. Bad weather is a big disadvantage as it limits our air power. Just before takeoff one of the pilot's unknown to us keyed his microphone and spoke: "I'm not sure if I want to fly with you two. It appears you guys are bullet magnets." A perfect hover and takeoff and off to Dak To we go. I couldn't help tease Dave with the bandage three times larger than the wound. "You're not going to take a Purple Heart just because you got shot in the head, are you?" I said with a grin. We arrived at Dak To airstrip on time, whatever time that was. Four of our 4th Aviation gunships would be part of today's support for our 4th Division Infantry on the ground.

Helicopter crews went home every night or at least back to the somewhat safe airfield while the infantry—the eleven Bravos (11B's military occupation)—or affectionally known as the "Grunts,"— ground pounders slept amongst their brothers with the enemy nearby doing the same. Those men have my deepest respect and admiration. They go days without sleep and are in constant danger of losing their lives. Oddly enough as it may seem, they would come over to us at our gunships and marvel at how crazy it must be to be a door gunner on a gunship. It guess it's all relative. Our 4th Division infantrymen have been in daily and around-the-clock contact with the NVA regulars since this campaign began ten days ago. They would not be going home tonight to a warm bed. I felt like I was cheating somehow. I enlisted in the Army and requested aviation as my MOS for that very reason. I did not want to be a "ground pounder." These guys were the real heroes of the war.

We landed and went straight to the fuel depot and topped off the fuel. We made sure our mini-guns, M60s and rockets were prepared for today's mission; it's what we do. It doesn't matter what hill we were trying to take, but the flavor of the day was Hill 723. Our mission was the valley north of 823 that was a supply and escape route. It really didn't matter if they shared every detail of a mission with us because we're just going to follow orders anyway. It was respectful if they did. Some pilots always did, some never did. They had discovered a trail that was a main supply line for the NVA near the Cambodian border, and after a heavy artillery barrage that was to take place at 0900 hours we would make a series of gun-runs on the trail with hopes of slowing the resupply of supplies for our enemy. There was a small village near the trail that was a suspected of serving as a holding area for NVA reinforcements. The best information we received was that there were no friendly troops there and that we were free to fire at anything and everything that moved. Firing on friendly troops was always a concern. It was bad enough the infantrymen faced "Charlie's bullets" but ours too? Our targets would be marked by smoke rounds sent by the artillery units positioned at a Special Forces firebase that would become well known by everyone in that area: Ben Het! That place was Hell on earth. Months later I would make frequent trips there for various reasons and learn that they were on guard 24/7 from rocket, mortar and sapper attacks.

We lifted off at 0915 hours and made our way to the target area. We saw little return fire on both of our sorties. We saw one aircraft go down and the almost immediate extraction by a rescue Huey and their brave crews that risked life and limb for the downed crew. First responders, as we know them today, are a special kind of people that didn't get the recognition back then as much as they do now. We still had one run left in our ammo, and as soon as the rescue was complete, we turned our gunships loose on the downed aircraft to destroy it. The equipment left behind and anything like the valuable radios or arms left behind could someday be used against us. We expended all of our rockets, mini gun, and M60 ammo and turned east for Dak To.

Upon landing, we refueled, rearmed, and stood ready for another possible mission. A hot meal was waiting for us on the runway—chicken and biscuits with green beans. Not like Mom's but better than canned ham and lima beans. We couldn't leave our ships, and with only C-rations on board the meal of alleged chicken and biscuits was pretty tasty and very much appreciated. The gun crews from the 17th Air Cav and 335 AHC unit made their way to the makeshift mess area. As we ate, shared our stories, jokes, and hometown locations, a loud voice erupted out of nowhere: "Put that God damn camera down, soldier!" All heads turned and focused on a helicopter approaching from the southwest of the airfield. Directly behind and temporarily concealing the Huey H model from our vision was the glare of a bright afternoon sun, making it nearly impossible to make out what provoked "Put that God damn camera down, soldier!" As the Huey approached, our eyes were spared the sun's glare as the aircraft and its cargo descended in preparation for landing. It was quickly becoming clear just why photographs were not a good idea. Underneath the aircraft was a huge, brown rope-cargo net. At first I couldn't see what the big deal was with this H model and its netted cargo. As the aircraft drew nearer, however, it became apparent why the camera operator was shut down. The "net" was carrying six, maybe eight, dead soldiers—our soldiers, our brothers.

Sons of American families were being transported in a net. A lump in my throat felt like a baseball. You could hear a pin drop. A few arms and legs of these young soldiers protruded through the rope net, making this way too real for a bunch of twenty-year-old kids. Most, if not all of us, turned away from this grotesque display of war flying toward us. I tried to think of something else, anything else, but I couldn't get that net out of my mind. I still can't. I heard later, though not confirmed, that they were from 4th Division Unit from Hill 823. These boys were gone forever. Their mothers and fathers would be notified shortly that Johnny wasn't coming home like he had promised. Every time I read this part, that baseball reappears in my throat.

We loaded up and prepared for one more sortie today. This time we were attacking a suspected enemy supply route west of Ben Het. But either they weren't there or they were concealed. No return fire was witnessed as we emptied four helicopter gunships in the area chosen by the powers to be. Air Force Phantom jets followed up with 500 lb bombs, and as we flew west we could feel the concussion those bombs produced.

Air Force/Navy jets, B-52's, artillery, helicopter gunships, tanks, advanced weaponry and all the technology available in 1967 was ours. What makes our enemy carry on with their desire to rid us of their country is hard to understand. The thought of our adversary's conviction, dedication and sacrifice to their cause is something I respect and think of a lot.

The net and what it symbolized is disturbing—wasted lives, hopes, family, and the American dream. Dak To was wearing us out and we could only hope that a big brown net slung under a helicopter wasn't our destiny.

We have been informed that we will be back tomorrow and probably the next day and the day after that. The icing is starting to melt off this cake.

Chapter 6

HILL 875

Being on these gunships felt like I was in an old Western movie that I watched as a young boy, especially when the Cavalry came charging over the hill, their bugles blaring and flags a' flying, and everything got better in a hurry.

≈≈≈

It's still November and it's still Dak To. We're going there again today. The weather is on our side once more as we sit waiting for the "ready, set, go" for takeoff. The airfield at Camp Enari is wall-to-wall helicopters of all shapes and sizes. Some are supplies, some are troops, but most are gunships belonging to the 17th Air Cavalry and the 335th AHC, affectionally called "Cowboys." These guys were in the thick of everything. They lost a few helicopters and the crews that manned them. It seemed odd that we weren't off the ground yet, but that reason was about to be revealed. Dak To was under a rocket and mortar attack. The fuel and ammo depots were hit providing a Fourth of July fireworks display that would burn and cook off rounds of ammunition for two or three days before burning out. A 4th Division Sergeant Major lost both arms in the blast while valiantly trying to save the much-needed ammunition. On this same day, two C-130 troop and supply aircraft were destroyed. Those two aircraft would be left at the end of the runway where they met their final end for a few days, reminding us of how quickly your life can be taken. Under such conditions we would be unable to re-arm or refuel, so we'd stationed for the next two days at Kon Tum, which was more than halfway to Dak To. That meant we could be there in minutes when needed. Those two aircraft would be left at the end of the runway where they met their final end for a few days reminding us of how quickly your life can change.

41

I was becoming very familiar with the Dak To area. We didn't go there every day, but I would guess we were there, or the surrounding area at least twenty or more days of the thirty-three days the battle went on. This mountain-laden area in the Kon Tum Province was detrimental to your health. Being alert could make the difference between life and death. The invading seven thousand plus PAVN/NVA soldiers are here, and they are no pushovers. They know the terrain and know how to use it to their advantage.

Thanksgiving is only a couple of days away. I recollected the family Thanksgiving Day dinners at Grampa and Grandma's house. I could smell the dinner and assortment of homemade pies that I hoped I could enjoy once again someday soon. The constant everyday battles at Dak To continued, and the severity of this situation worsened day after day with no end in sight. We have been coming here since around the 9th of November. Many hours would pass when we would be on standby sitting on or near the runway waiting for an assignment that never came. Sitting on a runway with the sun beating down on us in 80□ weather made for a bad day, but it was nothing in comparison to what those boys out there were having to deal with, fighting for hills with numbers that no one cared about. There was always artillery activity taking place, and often in the distance we could hear the explosions of B-52 strikes that shook the ground even though they were miles south of us. The B-52s accounted for over 250 air strikes in November of 1967 at Dak To. Most Vietnam vets would come to know those strikes as "arc lights." Grid co-ordinates would be given, and you better be out of that area or you would be rained upon with over 50 bombs ranging in weight from 500 to 750 lb. Forty helicopters would be lost or damaged enough to be put out of commission. Most of our missions were to hit military supply routes that provided supplies, reinforcements and escape routes for the enemy. We would sometime empty our gunships of ammo without seeing any proof of accomplishment for our efforts. The element of surprise gave us an advantage on these sorties, and little return fire was expected or received. I wouldn't fire my gun in any other direction than the paths of our rockets unless I was told to do so.

Hill 875, although only one of the many hills fought for, would be the battle most remembered for the loss of over 20 killed and another 30 wounded due to a friendly-fire incident. A Marine pilot dropped a 500 lb bomb in the middle of the command center where the wounded, medics and command groups were located. It has long since been determined that the pilot of that jet bomber was given the wrong coordinates by someone on the ground. What could be worse than killing one of your own? I can't imagine how bad the pilot must have felt when he learned of the tragic event. All toll, Hill 875 claimed the lives of 115 brave young men and 253 wounded in just a few days.

The 173rd Airborne (aka Sky Soldiers) were highly trained young men, and although they were good at what they do, they were ill-prepared for what they would find waiting for them in the Central Highlands. The terrain is rugged and jagged, with a triple canopy cover hiding a well-trained, fierce enemy that was dug in, experienced, and waiting for us. The 335 AHC Aviation group, also known as the Cowboys, were also good at what they do, and they were very busy supporting those Sky Soldiers that were in the thick of it on Hill 875. During what little time they had to rest, eat and refuel, they would give us updates on what was going on south of us at Hill 875 and neighboring hills.

It's November 22nd, the day before Thanksgiving. As we flew into Dak To, it was pretty obvious where the ammo dump used to be. Still smoldering and blackened from previous days of attacks, its location was easy to spot from the air. Every few minutes you could hear small explosions and bullets cooking off, which made us just a little bit jumpy! The two C-130's that were destroyed rested peacefully at the end of the runway and out of the way. We had been given the assignment of hitting heavily traveled NVA supply routes, and again the element of surprise was usually in our favor, that is, until about 1500 hours that day. We were re-armed, refueled, and fed by an army of mess cooks and KP troops. I don't recall the food that was served other than it being hot and accompanied by a warm beer (sometimes cool) in a rusty can. I don't know where the chocolate cookie came from, but it hit the spot.

On liftoff, I looked behind us and counted eight gunships and three more ahead of us. Our target was near one of the Special Forces firebases that was blocking the NVA's retreat. The NVA west of Dak To were in a retreat and in regroup mode and desperate to do just that. The pilots gave us their get-ready signal, so we locked and loaded our M60s and prepared once again to do what we had done so many times before. Six of the gunships that had taken off with us only minutes before banked to the north of us and disappeared in a valley below us. Straight away they commenced unloading their deadly cargo. The remaining ships, including ours, set sail for an area that was covered in smoke and fire from an obvious artillery barrage. We fired rockets from our pods, signaling that the attack was on.

We had caught a large element of NVA crossing an opening near a small river. All Hell broke loose. Green tracers were streaking everywhere in the sky. Dave and I were busy aiming at the rocket's direction and didn't notice holes appearing like magic in our floor's thin skin. Our ship took several hits as did the lead gunship, which was now smoking and obviously in danger of going down. The smoking gunship broke out of our wagon-wheel formation and headed back in the direction of the Dak To airfield. A whistling noise was coming from our rotors and a vibration was getting worse. I kept looking out the right door hoping to not see pieces of our ship falling off. My flight helmet's plastic shield kept falling down, and I kept trying to locate the knob, but it was gone. Panic raced through my mind as I thought for sure we were going down. WO Skinner keyed up and told Dave and me to lighten the ship—NOW! We started throwing out anything not bolted down, including our M60s and remaining ammo. We had our M16's and 38 caliber pistols available in case we went down before we reached safety.

The skill of our pilots was about to be put to the test of their lives and mine. Engine power seemed fine but the ever-growing loud, whistling noise and vibration were not good signs. These Bell Aircraft Company UH 1 helicopters, affectionately known as Hueys, were pretty durable, and it took a pretty good hit to bring one down.

The Dak To airfield was not far ahead of us, and as we drew closer and started the final few hundred feet descent, I felt as though I could breathe again. The touchdown was a little rough, but we were on the ground. The rotors were still in motion when Dave and I jumped from the ship. As the rotors came to a stop, so did the whistling sound that had originally signaled the start of this terrifying event. The pilots got out quickly but not as quickly as Dave and I. Fire extinguishers were ready but not needed. A change of underwear was probably a better idea. The first gunship that was hit ahead of us and that limped back to the airfield was smoldering and obviously severely damaged. Medics were working feverishly to attend to a crew member who seemed lifeless. Others worked in earnest to remove a badly wounded pilot from the cockpit as an emergency crew sprayed fire retardant where an apparent fire danger existed. We never—I mean never—made it a point to stare or gape, and we quickly turned our attention to our situation at hand.

The whistling noise had been caused by air passing through the perforated rotor blades, a dozen bullet holes, maybe more. Another four or five holes in the floor gave notice that the enemy shot back at us this time and didn't miss. Warrant Office Daily took a bullet in his left leg just below his knee, and he was in a great deal of pain. He was taken immediately to the aid station. He never returned to 4th Aviation that I know. That bullet gave him a ticket home. Dave looked at me rather oddly and asked me, "What happened to your helmet?" I replied, "Huh?" It came clear the reason my helmet visor kept falling down. An enemy bullet had creased my helmet, taking the visor knob clean off. We had just been issued these ballistic helmets that couldn't stop a direct bullet hit but could deflect one at thirty degrees or more.

After a thorough inspection, it was determined that our Huey was unfit to fly and would have to be taken back to Camp Enari for repairs—again! No matter, a few days away from here would be welcomed. As it turned out over forty helicopters would be lost in this November nightmare. I never heard how many airmen were lost, but knowing that forty choppers were shot down, there was no doubt more than a few airmen were lost.

We've been coming to Dak To since November 9th, not every day but at least twenty of them as I noted earlier. We are in the air almost every day with the exception of down time due to repairs. A few days we had convoy duty, a very boring mission. We would fly ahead, behind and over the truck convoys transporting supplies to Dak To, warding off any attacks from the NVA. We overheard the pilots saying that Hill 875 is in the final stages of being taken, and other than chasing the retreating NVA back north or into Cambodia, it was pretty much over . . . or so I thought!

Both of our pilots were hitching a ride back to Camp Enari. Dave and I were to stay overnight with our ship until a CH-47 arrived in the morning to hook our broken gunship back home. We gathered around a bunch of other crews from the 335th ATC and the 1st Air Cav as the sun began to disappear over the mountain's due west of the airfield. One of the Air Cav guys claimed to have been shot down four times. Another rookie blurted out, "I'm on my fifth ship this month." I looked around this bunch of guys from all over the United States and realized I was in the company of some pretty brave, young men.

We stayed up most of the night talking about cars, girls and, of course, some of the horrors we'd seen here at Dak To: burning helicopters, medevacs shot down while taking our wounded to safety. We prayed the crews were safe. More than one conversation revolved around the accuracy of the Air Force, Navy and Marine jets delivering bombs, napalm and their 20 mm mini-guns.

I often wondered what makes the enemy carry on knowing the firepower we possess. Eight-inch howitzers that are accurate up to twenty-six miles amazed me. B-52 bombers turned landscape into moonscape, and their thundering rumble was furious and deafening. Nobody brought up the infamous "net" from a few days ago, and I wasn't about to mention it.

We slept in our gunship that night cuddled up in a borrowed Army blanket on a cold metal floor. It had been pretty hot that day, but generally the nights would get down in the 50☐ range. One of the Air

Cav guys found a case of beer, and I broke out some crackers I had brought along. We sat around and discussed what we would have done if we were in charge. The sky was clear and dark. The stars seemed within arm's reach. I guess we got to sleep around 0200 or 0300 hours.

The morning arrived before we knew it, and at 0600 hours a row of gunships was ready to disembark. Dave and I could only watch as they made their way south to the awaiting target— Hill 875. I know now it was the last day of heavy fighting. It's Thanksgiving Day and although I'll miss the festivities at Grandma's, I'll never forget this particular day. I say a prayer each Thanksgiving Day for those boys. I would try to explain to my family what I was doing, but it somehow got lost in translation. We spent the morning and early afternoon sitting in our broken aircraft watching other helicopter gunships re-arm, refuel and some even had their turkey delivered to them when possible. We had Thanksgiving dinner that day on the airfield, and considering the circumstances, it was pretty darn good.

My Dak To experience was over for now. In a couple months I would be back here again for a number of weeks with my original unit—4th DIVARTY Aviation. Off in the distance a CH 47 (Chinook) was approaching to extract our wounded gunship and take us back to Camp Enari. It couldn't have taken more than thirty minutes after they landed that our ship was hooked up and ready to go.

We climbed aboard the Chinook for our ride home, and as we flew south to Camp Enari I felt a sense of relief and accomplishment. I thought, *I'm still twenty-years old and alive.* Not so fortunate, however, were 376 KIA and over 1440 wounded. Back home those families would be soon receiving a visit from a military representative delivering the bad news—no, the worst news.

I believe we spent approximately twenty days at Dak To and in the surrounding mountains. We flew countless gun-runs, lost two of our rides, two pilots and two crew members wounded and one boy from Henrietta, New York wondering, *What's next?*

Chapter 7

SKINNY SOLDIER

You didn't have to know anything about someone you saw lying there dead. I didn't even have to know his name. The cold, hard fact is that it could be me lying there.

≈≈≈

It's early December, and for the next few days we would be flying out of the firebase at Duc Co. Only a month earlier Duc Co was my first gun-run that scared the be-Jesus out of me. What few troops remained from the NVA's troop force from the November fight at Dak To were still fleeing to nearby Cambodia. Our damaged gunship from November 22nd was not reparable, so we were assigned a UH-1C model that was faster due to more horsepower and wider rotor blades. This extra power, lift and speed enabled us to carry more mini-gun ammo and ammo for our bungee corded, door-hung M60s. The excitement and adrenaline rush of going on a fire mission had somewhat waned by now. I had come to the realization that somebody was trying to kill my mother's son. I stopped sending letters of my whereabouts to my mother after my sister Mary Lou told me Mom was worried sick when on the news she heard the very name of the war zone that I had just told her I was stationed at, describing in-depth death tolls and the severity of the action.

December weather was typically pretty good. I don't recall getting rained on the past couple months, and I'm OK with that. A 4th Division Infantry patrol had been ambushed that morning, and our job was to strike the enemy near the Cambodian border. Two years ago, a major offensive took place here by the PAVN (NVA) known as the Battle of Ia Drang Valley. The movie that portrayed the battle, *We Were Young*, starred Mel Gibson as Lieutenant Colonel Hal Moore. The conflict was the first major battle between American troops and the PAVN (People's Army of Vietnam). On this day I was flying with Crew Chief Jerry Frimmel from Seattle, Washington. On the way to Duc Co our pilot took us through the very valley where the Ia Drang battle had been fought, and we were amazed by all the deserted bunkers that we saw. There was little or no foliage to hide them, apparently as a result of a defoliant later to be known as Agent Orange being sprayed, making it easy for us to find our foe in a barren landscape.

It's now about 1000 hours. Our gunship refueling was now complete, and our pilots left us to have a smoke and C-Rations while they attended a briefing on our day's upcoming mission(s). I don't recall the crew's names from the other gunship that made this trip with us, but one of them spotted a Huey flying directly at us erratically. "What the Hell is he doing? Something's wrong, very wrong," I heard someone shout. That Huey pilot landed hastily near us and my crew-mate Frimmel and I ran toward the now grounded aircraft as fast as we could. The rotors were still spinning when one of the pilots screamed that his co-pilot and one of his crew had been shot. A tall, skinny door gunner was slumped forward, lifeless but with no visible blood revealing a wound. Frimmel climbed onto the Huey, released the door gunner's safety belt, and the aforementioned soldier fell forward into another crew member's arms and mine. Frimmel joined us as we held the skinny soldier's head while searching for a reason for this limp, lifeless body. Jerry Frimmel, a Seattle native, unbuckled the flight helmet and proceeded to remove it by placing a thumb under each side of it and then lifting the helmet off the skinny soldier. What happened next was not for the faint of heart. The pressure of the tight-fitting helmet now removed released a gush of blood and brain matter on all who were nearby. Two of the closest crew members turned away, throwing up their previously eaten C-Rations. The smell was exactly the same as the odor given off when you clean a fish. My dry heaves and gagging were overwhelmed by the skinny kid's crew member shouting, "Oh my God! Please God, no!" Skinny's pilot was busy getting his co-pilot, who had been wounded, out of his chair and was not yet aware of the skinny soldier's brain matter being deposited on his unsuspecting rescuers.

Medics arrived, loaded up the wounded copilot, and then turned their attention to the crew member. The pilot saw what we had already seen and fell to his knees with his hands covering his face hoping that maybe this didn't really happen. It was probably only a short time ago before the two pilots and two crew members on this Huey were thinking about anything other than what was now happening. This war was ending lives and there was no warning.

Our now briefed pilots were running full speed to our ready gunships, yelling as they got nearby. "Load up . . . now!" We left the skinny soldier with the medics and quickly climbed aboard our craft. As the whirring whine of our turbine engines gained necessary power, WO Casey keyed up and told us we had the exact location of the enemy that had shot at skinny kid's aircraft. As we reached the end of the runway and achieved lift, I couldn't help but think that this was getting pretty personal. We weren't airborne five minutes before we arrived at the suspected enemy location. A pair of B40 rockets and those all too familiar green tracers came at us from the right—my side of the ship. Jerry and I dropped red smoke grenades to mark the spot where the rockets came from. The pilot turned a hard left and made as short as a half-circle a gunship can make in an effort to return to the billowing red smoke before they could get away. Our two gunships made two complete runs, expending everything from our mini-guns, bungee-corded M60s, M40 grenades and hand-dropped frag grenades on our red smoked mark. With no ammo remaining we headed back to the Duc Co airfield to re-arm. Passing us on the way were two gunships from the 1st Air Cav. They were on their way to avenge the loss of one of their crew members. Soon after, shells from a nearby firebase ravaged the hillside with 105- and 155-mm Howitzers.

The airfield came into sight, and so was the Huey on which the wounded co-pilot and the skinny soldier met their destiny. We would find out days later that the pilot survived his wounds and the skinny soldier lived as a vegetable for two days before passing. He was a short thirty days from going home. The story goes that he had met a Vietnamese girl and had just received orders that included taking her home with him. I don't recall his name, but I'm sure it's on that wall in Washington, D.C. Even if I did know his name, I wouldn't reveal it here as I wouldn't want a sibling to know how their brother died. The fact that he was never coming home was bad enough.

An infantry patrol made their way into the area we had attacked later that afternoon and there they discovered tunnels and fortified bunkers. They found several bodies of freshly killed NVA soldiers and a cache of assorted weapons. There were plenty of drag trails that gave evidence of bodies being dragged and hidden. They would do this so we could not count them as a KIA. I thought for sure we'd being going back there after re-arming, but we were done for the day. We were instructed to stay on the airfield that night, sleep in the ship, and be ready at, what else, 0600 hours.

No one got much sleep that night for a lot of reasons, and 0600 hours came quickly enough. We went up to a mess hall for breakfast and then returned to our ships. We sat there until after 0800 hours when the pilots returned and informed us that we were heading back to Camp Enari. Our presence here was no longer needed as the 1st Air Cav unit would arrive shortly to replace us.

With a few exceptions, major enemy activity in our area was light for the remainder of the December. We flew quite a few truck-convoy protections and LRRP (Long Range Recon Patrols) rescues. However, there was an apparent buildup of NVA soldiers and supplies just over the border into Cambodia. Those in the know thought that a major offensive could be in our near future. The will and determination of our enemy is pretty incredible.

Meanwhile, we got word today that Bob Hope would be at Camp Enari on December 27th. We could only hope that our enemy would give us a break and let us attend the show. My mother had sent me a letter in late November wanting to know if we had a tree for Christmas. I couldn't help but chuckle when I replied, "They don't have pine trees here, Mom." Mattel Toy Company provided us with dolls, baseball bats, balls and gloves for a local village. They asked for volunteers to bring the gifts there Christmas Day. Our entire flight group chose to do just that. Those children who barely had any clothes got Chatty Kathy Dolls, baseball bats, gloves and balls, and pull toys that made the sound of farm animals. It seemed like we didn't know how to act. Food and clothing might have been a better choice of gifts. Despite that, we had fun playing ball and taking our minds off those past few weeks.

On or about December 20th, a young officer entered our hooch and called out my name. I acknowledged that I was him. I was instructed to follow him. When we got outside, we approached a canvassed Army green truck. The officer said, "I don't know who you know in New York State, but this Christmas tree belongs to you." I must have looked dumbfounded as I read the attached card. "Compliments of New York Congressman Frank Horton." Huh! My mother had gone to his office and lobbied for a tree for her son. It was a real pine tree wrapped in plastic. It was a bit embarrassing, but when I brought it inside, I got more "wows" and "all rights" than if I just hit a home run in a World Series game. Everyone chipped in with something and it was decorated in about an hour. Every day someone would add some shiny object. Someone else got a small artificial tree, but all the good stuff went on my tree. December also saw a sharp increase in "care packages." I was getting almost a box a day. The best things were canned puddings, cookies, fudge and Kool Aid . . . lots of Kool Aid. I had so much Kool Aid I gave boxes to the mess hall for everyone to enjoy. The best box was my grandmother's orange-drop cookies. When I opened them, they were still warm! They must have been in the sun, but for that moment Grandma sent me warm cookies.

The Christmas Day truce was in effect, and for the most part it appeared to be honored by both sides. In retrospect the VC and NVA would adhere to this truce, so when their upcoming Tet truce occurred, our forces could only assume they too would honor a ceasefire.

The big day had arrived. On December 27, 1967, Bob Hope and Raquel Welch arrived at Camp Enari. Security was increased in and around the base. There would be thousands of GI's all in one spot. The

Army couldn't be too careful. Sgt. Barry came into the hooch about 0900 hours and said, "Boys, I'm sorry, but I need a volunteer."

Everyone moaned. "Sarge, it's Bob Hope Day," we cried out.

"I'm sorry, fellas, but if no one volunteers, I'll pick someone." Silence fell over us. You could hear a mouse piss on a ball of cotton! Sgt. Barry made eye contact with all of us as we awaited the sacrificial lamb to step forward. He announced that if someone didn't step forward real soon, he was going to pick one of us. Moments passed. Then the countdown began. Bingo! Sgt. Barry pointed at Gary Diescher from Alton, Illinois. "Come with me," he said. Of course, Gary was bummed and to no avail begged Sgt. Barry to pick someone else. Everyone else was elated.

"Better him than me" someone said. The sighs of relief spread like wildfire. Poor Gary! We went to the outdoor theater hours early to get good seats on the dirt hill, and on arrival we were stunned to see that about two thousand GI's had beat us to the punch. "Good thing we brought binoculars," someone said. About an hour after arrival, hundreds more GI's appeared, and I could only guess that there was a crowd of three thousand or more.
Richie from the Albany, New York had the binoculars, and in a sudden outburst he yelled out,

"You gotta be kidding me. Look, it's Diescher, and he's driving a Jeep. Oh my God, he's driving the Jeep that Raquel Welch is in."

Everyone wanted those binoculars, every one of us realizing it could have been one of us. The sea of thousands of GI's erupted with cheers when Bob Hope and Raquel Welch appeared on stage, and there was Gary, basking in the joy of chauffeuring Raquel Welch. As always, Bob Hope delivered a great show for entertainment-starved GI's in a theater of war.

When we got back to the hooch, we all waited anxiously for Diescher to return. The door opened and here he comes, strutting like a peacock. He first looked the other way as if to hide something, but then he suddenly looked straight at us, and low and behold he had the most beautiful lipstick set of lips you've ever seen. Raquel Welch had planted the perfect set of lips on Gary's cheek. He didn't wash his face for days, and every chance we got we would chase him, hold him down, and kiss those lips. Those moments were few, but they were good moments and became good memories. The brotherhood that would link all of us together someday and that would not be realized until decades later was growing right in front of our eyes and we didn't even know it. The skinny soldier was but one of many we left behind—a brother lost but not forgotten. He is a brother forever.

≈≈≈

In 1977 I was working at Del Webb's Townhouse as night-time security. The Phoenix Open Golf Tournament was in town. The hotel had quite a few celebrities staying there for the Pro-Amateur Golf event. It was about 2:00 a.m. and the lobby was empty except for me and a cute, little receptionist who I happened to be flirting with. That was when the elevator door opened. After a double take, maybe more, I recognized the man as none other than Bob Hope who was now walking toward us.

"I was hoping you had an aspirin," Mr. Hope said to me.

"Yes sir," I said. (Remember the little tins of Bayer Aspirin?) I reached behind the counter, picked out an aspirin and handed it to him with a glass of water. He said, "Thank you." Before he could turn away, I said, "Mr. Hope, I saw you at Camp Enari on December 27th with Raquel Welch. I know you've heard this before Mr. Hope, but I just want to say "Thank you, sir." He swallowed his aspirin, handed the glass back to me and said, "Young man, it was my pleasure, Thank you!" As he was getting on the elevator the young receptionist looked at me and asked, "Who was that . . . one of the golfers?"

Chapter 8

BAN MÊ THUỘT

Union General and future President Ulysses S. Grant was once quoted as saying, "War is Hell." *Of the 3,400,000 Vietnamese killed during the war, civilians accounted for 2,000,000 or 58 percent of all deaths of North and South Vietnamese. It was sure Hell for them.*

≈≈≈

The last few days of December, including New Year's Eve, were uneventful to say the least. Flying on gunships over hostile NVA forces in the Central Highlands and having uneventful days were OK for me. There were plenty of reports from LRRP's that the NVA forces were collecting near the borders of Laos and Cambodia, and a potential major offensive was a distinct possibility. Two other gunships and two slick Hueys (UH 1 D or H model often called the 4-door model) and crews had been in and out of Camp Enari all day extracting LRRP patrols that had made enemy contact. LRRP patrols typically consisted of only five heavily camouflaged and lightly armed crazy guys that were dropped off in areas to report on enemy activity. They would only engage when discovered, and we were involved in many extractions at any and all hours of the day and night. These guys were amazing. I couldn't imagine getting dropped off in hostile territory for days at a time. They loved us because . . . you got it . . . we were the *extractors.*

We returned to the hooch after evening mess and were notified that we were on twenty-four-hour "reaction" call and that we were not to leave the hooch unless so ordered. I had been on this call once or twice before and only lost sleep for my effort. When the call came, we would have to run to the operations hooch, grab our armor, flight helmet, ammo box and M60 and be on the ship by the time the pilots were buckled in and ready to go. Nighttime extractions were the worst.

57

Without being able to detect colored smoke in the dark we would count on radio and flashlight directions that were less than perfect and downright dangerous. In early December 1967, the LRRP's were outfitted with a new hand-operated strobe light distress light that would project the bright pulsating light for miles. This light made dark night extractions somewhat safer.

It's 2100 hours, January 1,1968. The hooch door explodes open and Sgt. Barry shouts at the top of his lungs: "Reaction team scramble, on the double. Move it." I have no idea what dream may have been rudely interrupted by these orders, but I was already dressed. I laced my boots and raced for the door. Halfway to our waiting gunship I realized I had forgotten my insulated flight jacket. I would regret this later. The weather was a little cool and with the doors wide open at a couple thousand feet elevation the forgotten jacket loomed large. We were headed to an area near Plei Me. Plei Me was near Duc Co and was always a hotbed of enemy activity due to the rugged terrain that made it difficult to root "Charlie" out of there.

As we approached the extraction site, the pilot from the leading Huey Slick made contact with the LRRP leader—Cowboy 6—below us. The LRRP team leader told the pilot they were a short distance from an open area and when he arrived, he would signal with his strobe distress marker or as we called it, the "candle." The two slicks and the three gunships circled the rendezvous area waiting for the strobe light to signal the exact location for pick-up. On our second lap a strobe light started flashing to our immediate right. The pilot acknowledged the marker was received and so they prepared for extraction. Cowboy 6 responded immediately: "Red Dog 1, our candle has not been lit. I repeat, our candle has not been lit." The lead slick pilot changed course immediately, avoiding the currently lit strobe light. We wagon-wheeled once more in an effort to determine which strobe light belonged to our LRRP team. "Cowboy 6, we have a problem. Another strobe is operating 400 yards to your north. Red Dog 1, our candle is now lit. I repeat, our candle is now lit." All at once a strobe light appeared, then another. There were now three strobe distress lights blinking. After a long pause, the Slick pilot now more than ever could not determine the LRRP team's location. "Cowboy 6, we now have three candles lit. It appears your friends down there have our equipment." Red Dog 1 keyed his microphone and gave the order: "Cowboy 6, would you mind going ice skating with me?" A moment of silence was followed by "Red Dog 1, I would love to." Watching all three strobes from a distance, I noticed two flashing strobes flashing wildly, and a third was making an unusual motion. It was a figure eight—a figure-skating figure eight. I thought, *Wow, that was brilliant!*

We had our target, and our Pilot WO Casey headed straight for the light first sighted. With our rockets and mini-guns directed at them, Dave and I opened fire on the first strobe light. Our red tracers lit up the sky, and the rockets glowed brightly as they headed for the intended target. The second and third gunship went for the second strobe light and emptied its armaments on them. We noticed little or no return fire. The dreaded green tracers were absent this night. After two complete gun runs, we were almost empty. A directive came down from the top ordering us to not totally use up our M60 ammo. The reason? If we were to get shot down, you will need those rounds to defend yourself and your crew members. They never set an amount on what to preserve, so we just took along a couple more belts. By then, the LRRP's were aboard the Slicks and heading for safety. The LRRP Patrol had lost one of their team, and at daylight an effort would be made to find him. I did hear that he was found days later near the sight of extraction. He had been hacked to death with a machete. These kinds of reports only made us hate our enemy more. During the excitement I paid little attention to how cold I was. But now that we were heading back, I closed the door as I was shivering and my teeth chattered. I was cold. I lit up a Marlboro and wished we were back already wrapped up in an Army green woolen blanket. I thought I'd never be warm again.

We landed, tied the rotor down, and because we were still on "reaction" call we had to rearm and refuel. It was 0300 hours and it was cold. We re-armed the rockets, loaded the mini-gun belts carefully in their tray, took our gear back to the operations hooch and hit the rack about 0500 hours. It was a long cold night. It felt good to get those 100 percent Army green woolen blankets on top of me. If we get scrambled again, I'll be taking one with me.

Numerous sources, including captured NVA soldiers, made it pretty evident that Charlie was on the move. Laos and Cambodia where off limits to U.S. forces, making those sanctuaries perfect to resupply, re-arm and replace those that were killed and wounded in the Dak To area only a short time ago. Something big, something really big was brewing. We were so often on the offensive, but it appeared the tables were about to be turned. A Special Forces camp near Plei Me was under threat of being overrun, and on the morning of January 7th we were summoned to that area. We would be staying at Duc Co and told to pack for a few days. The memory of the skinny soldier was and will always be connected to that place.

On arrival we landed but a few feet from the very spot we had made our futile attempt to aid the young, skinny American. We quickly refueled and were en route to Ple Me when we were diverted to a Montagnards village where NVA soldiers were reported to be hiding supplies and weapons. Montagnards are indigenous peoples of the Central Highlands of Vietnam. The French term Montagnard means *people of the mountain* and is a carryover from the French protectorate period in Vietnam. To make things more difficult, we were dealt a blow when an order came down that all villages are now designated as "no fire zones." Regardless of what we saw, no matter the circumstance, we were not to fire our ordnance within a certain radius of any and all villages.

A well-traveled trail on the western end of the village was suspected of being used by the NVA to transport supplies and possibly storing them in this no-fire zone village. It didn't take long to get there, and once there our two gunships and two others from an unknown unit circled clockwise around the village at a safe distance looking for clues. I'm not sure who noticed it first, but there were uniformed NVA soldiers inside the village in clear view of those on the right side of our ships. They obviously knew we couldn't fire into the village and they flaunted it. Whatever pilot was in command of this mission radioed to those in the know on whether there were any friendly soldiers that could possibly be in this village. Minutes went by as we awaited a reply.

On gunships you never really know if your bullets have actually found your target or not. Usually confirmed kills of that nature are at best a guesstimate or given to the company or unit involved, rarely to an individual. On our fourth pass around the village, we received word that there were no friendlies there, but the no-fire orders were still intact unless fired upon. The center of the village probably now contained twenty-five or more enemy soldiers. There was an absence of villagers, and I heard the discussion that they had either left their village or were killed by the NVA owing to their hatred of Montagnards and often killing them if they resisted.

Our pilots gave the lock-and-load order and told us to stand by. The pilots tightened the circle, and then all of a sudden, the order came. The no-fire order had been lifted. We were now commanded to fire at will. My crew mate Dave had come to my side of the aircraft with his M60 only minutes before. My M60 was loaded with solid tracer rounds, and through practice I got pretty good at walking rounds to the target. At the moment of the fire-a-will command, I fired multiple twenty-round bursts into the center of the village. Dave, in a frenzy to do the same, yelled out that my rounds had found their target, later claiming that he saw three or four NVA fall as a result of my efforts. The other right-side gunners of the follow-up ships did the same. This all took place in just five minutes or less. The four gunships now organized the attack with rockets and mini-guns, and one after another we assaulted the fleeing enemy. While all this was going on, an infantry unit was being airlifted to the site. Our guns now empty, we turned away and headed for Duc Co, leaving our infantry to finish what we started. Four more gunships passed us heading to where we had just emptied our ordnance.

My head was spinning from the adrenaline rush that would linger for hours. When we landed, my back was slapped and hand shaken to death. I got a lot of "Atta boy" and "Wow." What a rush. The next morning, feeling the pain of a couple too many beers and shots from my buddies, I heard tell that the NVA unit was beaten up pretty bad. The infantry unit found a dozen bodies and, as always, plenty of drag trails. But most important they found plenty of weapons. Worse than that, the NVA had killed the village chief and many villagers when they most likely objected to the NVA using their village to store their supplies. What on earth makes man do what he does to his fellow humans is mind boggling.

I only have a week or so remaining with this unit as my ninety-day, temporary duty stint was coming to an end. As much as I felt a part of this unit, I was starting to feel vulnerable. Going back to DIVARTY Aviation and not having an OH-23 of my own would make me available for menial tasks, and after Dak To and other events I would be quite bored, to say the least. We stayed at Duc Co another few days chasing "Charlie," extracting LRRP's and flying gun support for supply and troop convoys. The NVA buildup was becoming more evident as reports flooded in about sightings and contact. One thing that was unusual was that it appeared the enemy was not interested in engaging our troops, confirming they were saving their resources for something else.

We returned to Camp Enari on January 15th for two days. Our gunship needed routine maintenance, and the day after that was completed we received orders that we would be assigned to a 4th Division unit at Ban Mê Thuột. (pronounced ban me to it). We arrived early morning and settled in awaiting an assignment. It appeared to be another hurry up and wait scenario. The pilots, Casey and Skinner, gave us the OK to go in to the secure city if we wanted, but warned us to not wander off the main drag. Stay together. We decided to get something to eat first and what a treat it turned out to be.

We entered an Air Force mess hall and couldn't believe how good the food was. Best of all they had milk, real milk. I hadn't had a real glass of milk in over six months. Better than that, they had chocolate milk. These Air Force guys know how to go to war. We finished our roast beef sandwiches, four glasses of milk and an ice cream sandwich, and off to Ban Mê Thuột we go. An Air Force guy gave us a lift into town. This place is spectacular. Moss lined trees, clean streets, sidewalks and well-dressed people. It didn't seem like Vietnam or a war zone to me or anyone else.

We found a really cool bar at the Imperial Hotel and settled in for a few drinks and a little dancing with some beautiful Asian women. "This is my kind of war," one of our guys shouted. We danced, drank, and partied for hours, something we hadn't done since we got here. One girl of French and Vietnamese descent was as beautiful as a woman could be. I think it might have been Gary Diescher (of Raquel Welch fame) that wanted to take her home with him.

Sometime after midnight our Military Police entered the Imperial Hotel and ordered us back to base camp immediately. Without hesitation we finished our drinks and skipped saying goodbye to the women on who we just spent a week's pay on. We were quickly ushered out to five-ton trucks and loaded on. Any GI wandering on the streets was ordered to climb aboard quickly. If they hesitated, the MPs would not hesitate to use force to persuade them. Something was happening, and when asked the MP's all of a sudden became deaf. We had no guns or sidearms as they were not permitted on nights out. The drive back to the compound took maybe ten minutes. Our pilots met us at the barracks where we would be sleeping and told us to stay dressed and be ready to fly at a moment's notice. They quickly explained that an enemy soldier was captured and told interrogators that enemy soldiers disguised as civilians had infiltrated the city and were hunting unarmed GI's. The four of us that went in to town had a few alcoholic beverages and needed to sober up quickly. We consumed coffee and more coffee along with some mess hall cookies.

It was a few minutes after 0300 hours. The compound sirens blared the warning of a rocket and mortar attack. We flew out of bed and raced for our gunships. The pilots were right behind us. The distinctive whine of the single-shaft turbine engine suddenly was overshadowed by the explosion of one, no two, now three explosions a couple of hundred feet away. Radar had picked up the location from where the rockets were launched, and so our two gunships and two from another unit were dispatched to that location. As we approached the target, they were still launching. The all too familiar green tracers were flying, but because of the dark moon-less night they weren't even close to us. But what they did was give us their exact location. The four weapons-laden gunships responded with eight mini-guns, eight door guns and a lot of rockets. The area lit up like the Fourth of July—secondary explosions, rounds cooking off and one hell of a fire. Before you knew it, it was all over.

There would be no more nights at the Imperial Hotel for us or anyone else on this trip. We'd be gone in a couple days, never to return. In a couple of weeks, the Tet offensive would bring death and destruction to Ban Mê Thuột. The NVA and VC were ruthless, murdering anyone who had given services or aid to the enemy, meaning us. One of the terrible atrocities they committed was what they did to those girls at the Imperial hotel. Gary Diescher returned to Ban Mê Thuột in mid- February and was devastated when he heard what they had done to the French-Vietnamese girl and the others.

The next day we were reassigned back to Camp Enari. As we lifted off the compound runway, I couldn't help but think how neat the City of Ban Mê Thuột was, and in a few weeks I found out the city and its people were beat up pretty good by the NVA/VC. WO Casey pointed out that the area we struck was a Michelin rubber plantation, and because we damaged it our government would have to pay restitution to Michelin.

Camp Enari came in to view, and after another perfect landing we took our gear to the operations shack and returned to the hooch where Sgt. Barry was waiting. Sgt. Barry informed me that my orders were being processed to go back to DIVARTY Aviation. My replacement had arrived, but I would remain here a few days. He asked me to keep myself available for standby in case of someone coming down sick or unable to fly. In the meantime, I could spend my time at the airfield helping technicians doing preventative maintenance on Hueys until my orders were finalized to go back to DIVARTY Aviation. In a lot of ways, I felt sad about leaving B Company gunships, but I was bound to be safer. I'll miss Sgt. Barry. I would see him at the airfield now and then, and he was always nice to me. He made me feel welcome and treated me like I had been there since day one. They were a great bunch of guys, and in a day or two I would be gone. Yet, they would not be forgotten.

The very next morning Sgt. Barry approached me about 0900 hours and asked me if I would be willing to do a flight with A Company. Their door gunner was sick and they needed someone in about an hour. "Sure," I said. I went back to my locker, grabbed my flight jacket and other flight essentials and made my way to the A Company flight line where I met a Lt. Murphy who introduced himself by his call name of Renegade 32. "We need to make two runs to Kon Tum. Did Sgt. Barry tell you what we were going there for?" he asked. I told him no. "You'll find out soon enough," he replied. That reply opened my mind to all sorts of imagined options, but I didn't expect what was about to unfold.

The day started cool with some clouds, but by day's end it was pretty nice. Believe it or not, but we met at the airfield at 0900 hours. Yes, not at the normal 0600 hours that seemed to be so popular. We took off and headed to Kon Tum. We landed at a makeshift hospital clearly marked with a Red Cross symbol on the series of large tents attached to a wooden building. The three landing pads were also clearly marked with a big Red Cross. As we approached and landed, a five-ton truck was waiting for us. The H model (Slick) Huey gently landed on the targeted Red Cross. The rotors came slowly to a stop, and that all familiar noise of the rotors passing through the air subsided. The five-ton truck backed up to a safe distance from the rotors, dropped its tailgate, and four young men proceeded to remove six black body bags of young men who had given all. The bags were placed within ten feet of our empty aircraft. The crew chief that belonged to the aircraft said, "C'mon, let's get them onboard." Five of the bags were heavy enough that we needed help from the other guys to help load them. The last bag was smaller and weighed about sixty pounds. One of the guys helping us told us this one was a door gunner who was shot and did not have his monkey strap on. The monkey strap was on all 4th Aviation ships. It was a six-foot webbed belt that was worn to keep crew members from falling out of the aircraft. The Sergeant in charge of this detail told us that he had been shot, fell from the aircraft, and went through a dense tree line tearing him to pieces. This sixty-pound bag was all that remained of him. That's all that was left of him to be sent home to his yet to be notified family.

We lifted off and made our way to Camp Holloway to drop them off at a KIA registration unit to prepare them for returning them home to their families. Having those six bags at my feet and knowing what they contained was an emotional moment, and my helmet and glass shield kept this flight crew from seeing the tears running down my cheeks. Please keep in mind that I use to cry watching *Little House on the Prairie*. We would make one more trip that day for the remaining four rubber bags. When we returned from our final delivery, I got off the aircraft, helped tie the rotor down and walked away without saying a single word. Nor did anyone else say a word. Days don't get much darker than this.

Chapter 9

ORRIN DYER

A close friend recently asked me if writing this memoir was a cathartic experience. I have never heard or seen this word before, so, I looked it up. Catharsis: providing psychological relief through the open expression of strong emotions; to purge, purify and cleanse.

≈≈≈

January was nearing its end, and I looked back and realized that it would be a month of transition for me. My last few days at B Company would be spent going on "normal" missions near the Cambodian border, guarding convoys, extracting LRRP's and trying to kill people. That is not normal! My 90-day TDY would end soon. Unusual happenings would often serve as a prelude of what was waiting for me the next couple of months. We often found the enemy would avoid contact as if to save themselves for something big. Every day we heard of the enemy buildup near the borders. B-52's were making daily "Arc Lights" on those areas. LRRP teams were being extracted daily as contact with the NVA became more frequent. Large concentrations of NVA signaled one thing: a major enemy offensive was drawing near. In about a week the Vietnamese New Year celebration (Tet) would certainly bring about a ceasefire like our recent Christmas Day ceasefire that was honored by both sides. Tết— Vietnamese New Year, Vietnamese Lunar New Year or Tet Holiday— is the most important celebration in the Vietnamese culture. Tet would soon be a word synonymous with treachery, and to this day when two Vietnam veterans meet and exchange their duty and time spent there, more often than not one will ask the other, "Were you there for Tet?" The previous and future Tet holidays carried none of the notoriety of the 1968 Tet offensive.

I said my goodbyes to my friends at 4th Aviation. My temporary duty there was complete. I'll miss these guys. We went through a lot together at Dak To, Duc Co, Ban Me Thout, not to mention the net and the skinny soldier. The replacements had arrived, and I was heading back to my original assignment at 4th HHB DIVARTY Aviation. I knew that going back there would be a safer place to be. I would soon learn the hard lesson to assume nothing. DIVARTY Aviation got rid of the old hooch, and we were now housed in a long wooden structure that had space for sixteen beds. We didn't have that many crew chiefs, so we shared space with a few clericals and a big black man, Joe Bob Miles. I don't even recall what his job was, but he would become my best friend in the 'Nam'!

I was summoned to Capt. Bacon's hooch the next morning. He had wished me well when I left DIVARTY and was about to welcome me back with a twist. After a salute and a handshake, he went on to say, "My pilots are glad you're back. You possess a different set of skills than the others here. If you didn't bring your M60 with you, then I will get one for you. Our pilots feel naked up there alone in those 23's. A few, not all, have asked if you wouldn't mind accompanying them on certain missions where an experienced combat crew chief could make a difference."

"Of course," I said assuredly.

Before I could say anything else, he told me I'd be going to Dak To and relieve Duke Albertson and crew of the OH-23 that Capt. Buckingham was piloting. He also informed me that in a few days I would be meeting CWO Orrin Dyer, another pilot who arrived only a few weeks prior to DIVARTY. Albertson was to stay with me a few days until I got the lay of the land and what was expected of me up there.

"Be ready to go after breakfast," he said. "Good to have you back."

"Thank you, sir. I'll be ready."

I was no stranger to Dak To and no stranger to the dangers that occur daily at this Hell on earth. I hitched a ride with Capt. Lyons since he was going there to bring some high-ranking officer back to

Camp Holloway. Capt. Lyons stayed with the aircraft waiting for his fare. I took my sleeping bag, extra clothes, flight helmet and M60 off the OH-23. Duke was at the airfield when I arrived and took me to the underground bunker that he and others had built. The bunker was pretty cool: eight feet underground and covered in another three feet of sandbags. It would sleep four and could withstand a mortar round or two, making it about the most secure place I would sleep in so far. I caught Duke eyeing my M60, and I could see a question brewing.

"What's with that thing?" he asked. "You know, the other crew chiefs are thinking that they will be expected to start flying with that thing, and they're not happy about it. Just because you're fucking nuts doesn't mean they are."

I replied, "Duke, the pilots don't expect the other crew chiefs to do that." Actually, not all the pilots want a gun on board. The gun and I will only go when a pilot asks and I am the only one they'll ask."

"We'll see about that," he said under his breath but audible enough for me to hear it. "C'mon, let me show you around. Don't go to the mess halls at the regular hours. The "dinks" launch their rockets and mortars at the mess areas when they see the troops heading for them. You're better off eating C-Rations here in the bunker or hit the mess halls before or after hours. Before I go back, you can help me build a shower. I got a bunch of wooden artillery ammo boxes from the artillery guys. We'll do it tomorrow."

"Sounds like a plan," I said.

Duke and I went to the flight line around 0700 to prepare the OH-23 for Capt. Buckingham in case they had him going someplace that day. We finished the pre-flight and went to a 4th Division Artillery mess tent for rubber eggs and greasy bacon. Duke had started the wooden box shower a few days ago, and by the end of the day we had it done. We hoisted the 55-gallon drum and emersion heater up, and about the time we finished, Capt. Lyons showed up and told Duke he was taking him back to Enari. Duke quickly gathered his stuff and rushed to the airfield for his awaiting taxi. I never saw Duke again as his tour ended in a couple of weeks.

Capt. Buckingham and I spent the rest of that day organizing our temporary home and sharing our stories about life back home, family and other stuff. He would only be here a couple of days until CWO Dyer arrived. Capt. Buckingham asked to be called Buck when he and I were together.

I did a pre-flight on the 23 while Buck was in a briefing. I wanted to finish the shower's plumbing and fill the barrel with water, but I would need help with that.

I was filling the Gerry cans with water when Buck showed up with map in hand and said,

"Let's go for a ride. Bring your p-shooter with you." *Cool,* I thought.

"Where we going?" I asked.

"Ben Het," he said.

Ben Het was a special forces camp north of Dak To and close to the border of Laos and the infamous Ho Chi Minh trail. It presented an unusual configuration. The Ben Het Special Forces there were always on guard. Anytime we flew in to Ben Het we never, and I mean never, shut down our aircraft. An FAC (Forward Air Controller) from a 4th Division Infantry unit met us at the Dak To airfield. Ben Het was getting mortared, and our job was to call in artillery in order to stop it. A short flight later as we approached the camp, we could see smoke rising from the east perimeter. The FAC and Buck went to work. Buck keyed up and told me to concentrate on any incoming tracers (green) and return fire. There were no friendlies in that area, so there was no danger of firing on them. Listening to the FAC giving map co-ordinates and instructions to the artillery unit was new to me. In a few weeks I would get to do the same. It took only two minutes before artillery rounds thundered. There is no noise I could make that could

70

duplicate the sound of artillery rounds screaming through the skies on their way to their target. Once I located where the artillery rounds were hitting, I opened up with the M60. I fired short 20 to 25 round bursts at my target while Buck maneuvered the OH-23 for a better look. The small tree-filled hilltop where the mortar rounds came from was now barren and smoldering. I continued firing on the fringes of the hill top for escapees from the barrage of artillery rounds.

The FAC keyed his microphone. "I like having your gunner with us."

We had not received any return fire that I could see. I'm sure Charlie was on a dead-run knowing those HE (High Explosive) artillery rounds were on their way. The FAC leaned forward, looked around Buck and gave me a thumbs up. I nodded a thank you back. Looking back east, it was obvious the mortars had ceased hitting Ben Het. Being onboard for one of these artillery events was new to me and pretty exhilarating, to say the least. Buck had no intentions of landing at Ben Het. He radioed the command center and asked if there was another fire mission. A few moments later the response came and we were released to return to Dak To. We returned without incident.

The refueling didn't take long as we were only airborne about an hour and a half. Hovering back to our revetment, I couldn't believe how much fun that was. Buck shut the 23 down, I unbuckled, got out, and as soon as the rotors came to a stop, I tied it down. Before I returned to the bunker, I logged the necessary information in the green log book kept under the seat. The FAC and Buck exchanged some conversation that was too muddled for me to understand. "I'll see you back home," I said. The FAC gave me a nod and said, "Goodbye." As I prepared to salute the young Lieutenant, he stopped me. "Hope to see you again, and thanks for coming along." *Wow!* I thought. They headed for the command center to file their report of the operation. I felt pretty good about the mission and felt I did what was expected of me.

On his return home from his debriefing, Buck helped me hoist the water-filled Gerry cans to the top of our brand-new shower. I filled the drip-gas can to our immersion heater with aviation gas and lit it.

"We should have warm water in about twenty minutes," I said. "Great," Buck said. "Me first," he added. Buck finished his shower and walked off as I readied for my shower." I'll be right back," he said. While I was showering, Buck went to the officers' mess tent and brought ham sandwiches back. I poured some Jack Daniels over a Coke and with that sandwich we had a good dinner. It's always a good ending to a good day when everyone gets home safely.

Buck was gone in a couple days but not before we performed a few more visits to Ben Het and the surrounding area. Surveying was a big part of our aviation operations: mapping trails, hills, and valleys that could be used for enemy forward observers, trails that troops could travel to enter an area or an escape route. I brought the M60 each time but never had an opportunity to fire it while with him. Buck warned me about CWO Dyer. He's not fond of having passengers, especially ones with guns. He's not one much for idle conversation either.

CWO (Chief Warrant Officer) Orrin Dyer arrived to take his turn at Dak To. I estimate that he arrived on January 28th. CWO Dyer was serious about what he did, and he wasn't the most talkative guy alive. At the ancient age of thirty-eight, he was one of the oldest pilots we had. We didn't have much of anything in common, so conversation consisted of a lot of small talk. He asked me why I wanted to be out forward like this. I told him I just wanted to do my part.

"I'm not sure I want a door gunner tagging along," he said. He felt my being there with an M60 hanging out the door might draw fire. "I'll do whatever you want," I replied.

In truth, most of the pilots wanted me onboard. Apparently, Orrin was not one of them. He did tell me he had three children and was from New Hampshire. That was all I'd ever know about him other than his obvious attention to detail and his focus on the task at hand.

~~~

January 31. I know this date well. At 0100 hours mortars and rockets are raining down on us from the mountains from the west and from the south. Artillery response was fierce. I could now relate to what the end of the world would sound like. The sky lit up with flashes from the 155 mm, 8 in, and 175 mm howitzers that responded immediately to the attack. CWO Dyer and a pilot from another unit who was spending the night with us sprung off their cots like they were in a hurry to go someplace. I locked and loaded my Car-15 and the M60, wanting to be prepared if the VC/NVA got through the wire. The assorted Howitzers were pointed point-blank range at the western hills. With each salvo our bunker shook and hunks of our dirt walls crumbled. We couldn't hear any small-arms fire which would indicate they had not breached the wire.

We didn't know it yet, but this was the beginning of the infamous Tet Offensive. Over one hundred assaults on U.S. bases and Vietnamese cities were being struck at the same time from the DMZ up north to the southern tip of South Vietnam. This explained the buildup of enemy forces in Cambodia and Laos and their obvious avoidance of contact. I am not surprised that Army Intelligence (an oxymoron) were unable to figure out that something like this was bound to happen with all the sightings and obvious clues. Even with the increased enemy contact we were not under extreme enemy pressure like other parts of Vietnam. All military bases and cities were on elevated alert or under attack. Pleiku and Camp Holloway were being hit pretty hard, although the beating the NVA took here at Dak To only a couple of months ago diminished the all-out effort they were carrying out nationwide due to their heavy losses they suffered here in November.

The artillery units were relentless in their defense of our base and the all-important airfield that was capable of landing all military aircraft necessary to bring in troops and supplies to thwart this all-out attempt by the NVA/VC to drive American forces from their country. CWO Dyer was in the air without me February 1 and 2, observing enemy positions. On February 2, CWO Dyer and the FAC spotted NVA spotters in an area they called "Rocket Ridge." It was a strategic spot for enemy spotters, having a clear and unobstructed view of our base, and as many times as they were cleared from the area by our artillery and F4 Phantom jets they would quickly return to guide the mortars and rockets to their final destination.

The F4 Phantom jets were incredible. They would fly over our bunker firing their 20 mm Gatling guns with a sound that was unbelievable. There was no distinguishable sound of one round being fired but a roar that only a Vietnam veteran could duplicate. Shell casings would rain down upon us as they unleashed their six barrel, 6,000 rounds per minute guns on the mountains west of us shortly followed by 500 to 750 lb bombs. I don't recall napalm being used at that time, but it was used on concentrated enemy troops extensively throughout the war.

On February 3, I readied our aircraft for CWO Dyer and a new FAC. I learned later that the FAC was Lt. Larry Skoglund. I don't recall what time it was, but I did my daily pre-flight on our OH-23 like I had done so many times before. I performed the magneto check, applied some power and lifted the collective stick to a point of almost a hover. I shut the 23 down and inspected the aircraft for fluids and important safety-wire inspection. Now the aircraft was ready to go. I filled out the log book, lit up a smoke, and looking out to the mountains west of us I was surprised that it was unusually calm based on the previous few days' events.

I can't 100 percent affirm that I met Lt. Skoglund since I never knew any of the FAC's because they were rarely the same one two times in a row. But as I passed CWO Dyer on my way. I invited myself to tag along, saying, "I'll be right back. I need to get my stuff."

"You can stay behind," WO Dyer replied. "We'll only be gone for about an hour on a short survey. I'm sure you can find something to keep you busy." Those would be the last words I would hear from Orrin Dyer. A couple of hours passed and still they had not returned. I was cleaning the bunker, taking out the garbage and raking the dirt floor when a Major appeared at the bunker opening. "Are you Warrant Officer Dyer's crew chief?"

"Yes, sir," I replied as I stepped up and out of the bunker.

"Warrant Officer Dyer and the FAC were shot down, and I'm sorry but they are both KIA."

A numbness took over at this point and I must have looked confused. The Major repeated what he stated only moments before and then continued with "I need you to collect any personal items and prepare them for return to Camp Enari. They had almost made it back and crashed just short of the runway. You'll also need to go there as well and collect any personal items from the aircraft."

In my numbed state I picked up the things he had left in the bunker, which consisted of a small photo album, unfinished letters and the normal stuff we all carried with us. I proceeded to the airfield expecting to see this crumpled OH-23 but was surprised to see this burnt-to-the-ground OH-23 that only hours ago I had prepared for CWO Orrin Dyer's last flight. It was still smoldering and both bodies had been removed. There was nothing there for me to collect. At this point I hadn't processed the dark thought that if it had been up to me, I would have been on that aircraft.

I don't recall which one of our pilots flew from Enari to collect the items, but he offered to take me back with him. I chose to stay there and deal with the horrific event and wait for the arrival of a replacement helicopter and pilot. Later that day I was told that Lt. Skoglund survived the return flight, having been shot and burned pretty badly. I tried very hard to find Larry over the years, but my efforts were to no avail.

Approximately forty-plus years later and after posting the story about the death of CWO Dyer on a 4th Division website, I gave out my phone number in case Larry might see it. The odds of hearing from him were definitely against me. Then a few days after posting the story my phone rang one evening. The phone number was unfamiliar and I almost didn't answer it. Out of curiosity I answered.

"Hello," the caller said. "Is this Paul? Paul, this is Larry." I couldn't believe this was happening. We spoke for an hour and agreed to meet someday. Two years later Larry called and said he was going to a reunion in Washington, D.C. We agreed to meet in Gettysburg, and there we had a nice dinner at Farnsworth House. I took my wife Carol back to the Quality Inn on Steinwehr Avenue. Then Larry and I had a couple of beers and sat on a bench until 2 a.m. talking about his ordeal. I expressed my guilt for not being with the crew that day and wondering if I could have made a difference.

Larry said, "Paul, it happened so fast that there was nothing that you could have done to change the outcome." He gave me the gruesome details that I have decided not to share here just in case CWO Dyer's family should read the account someday. Larry spent a year in a hospital for his wounds and burns from the crash while he made a valiant effort to get the OH-23 back to the airstrip. It was all pretty remarkable considering the condition of the aircraft. Prior to Larry's surprise phone call, I had made contact with Orrin's daughter. I shared that contact with Larry, and he met with her in Kansas City sometime later.

≋

The following is Larry Skoglund's abbreviated account of Feb 3, 1968:

I was returning from R & R in Sydney, Australia. On the flight back I knew nothing of the Tet Offensive going on in Vietnam. The Australian news was full of details about the U.S. spy ship *Pueblo* that had been captured off the coast of North Korea, but nothing was being reported about Vietnam or Tet!

Walking through the little "terminal" at Dak To, we ran into the brigade air officer who was more than a bit agitated.

"Skoglund," he shouted, "you've got to get up in the air right now and help with artillery support. Now! A helicopter is idling right here waiting for an observer." But I had a slight problem with this simple request: I was in my khakis, no boots, no flight helmet with the mic, no maps, nor my M16.

"Here's a flak jacket, and oh. . . . there are no electronics on this OH-23. It's been red tagged but these guys need help." These guys were an infantry patrol five kilometers off the west end of the airstrip that had run across some NVA. They had no way to talk with any artillery unit, nor could they reach their unit for help. I'd been an FO (Forward Observer), seen plenty of combat, and also been engaged in combat where we couldn't get artillery support. It quickly became clear to me how critical this mission was.

The OH-23 pilot was WO Orrin Dyer. Although I had met WO Dyer before, I did not know him well since most of my aerial work was with fixed wing L-19s. I grabbed two radios—backpack types PRC10. One of the radios had the DIVARTY radio frequency and the other with the endangered infantry's radio frequencies. I had a topographical map and a compass the liaison had passed to me, so I nodded to WO Dyer and strapped in. We flew five minutes due west and started looking for the infantry patrol. We were flying low (more to keep the NVA from seeing us coming than anything else) and not too slow, doing some wide circles. Almost right away I spotted a uniformed NVA and turned to give WO DYER a shout. At that moment all Hell broke loose. The bubble was perforated with bullets, and I had my right arm shattered as it was extended, holding the map. I very seldom wore a flak jacket, but on this rare occasion I did. They were very clunky, heavy and awkward. But this one probably saved my life because the bullet wound was right in line with my chest. I hollered and looked at WO Dyer. He was slumped in the seat with a fatal wound to his lower jaw. I couldn't move my arm; it was just hanging there. The lower bones had been blown apart along with the tendons, muscles, nerves and artery. I was bleeding badly, and I knew I could not squeeze my upper arm to stop the blood flow. I immediately grabbed the right stick with my good arm and locked the one between my legs with my knees. I knew we had to get out of there somehow. We were low enough so the jungle canopy prevented more shots at us. I knew the rudiments of what went on to control the thing. Throttles were set and not moving, foot pedals controlling the tail rotor that determined our direction. Slowly pushing the left pedal, I got us aimed at the airstrip, which I could see in the distance. I couldn't do much with the stick (cyclic) between my knees, but we were moving forward. I concentrated on the one in my left hand (collective) that controls the up/down or the pitch of the blades. In a very erratic manner I was returning to the airfield. I had no intention of attempting a set-down near anything and planned on hitting the dirt on either side. As we got near the runway, I got really tired, weary and passed out from the blood loss. I can clearly recall saying to myself, "Fuck it, this is too much work." That's when I blacked out. The last thing I remember was a brilliant white light filling my head. I was told later by a Lt. Plager that the OH-23 all of a sudden went straight up and fell backward to the ground and exploded.

I vaguely recall a fellow dragging me to a three-quarter ton truck and fighting to get me in the seat. He took me to the triage medical unit on the runway, and I think I heard them mumbling while cutting off my khakis. I was burned on the left side of my face, my left arm and left leg, along with the gunshot wound. According to my records, I was given morphine and blood plasma. I next awoke in the 71st Evac Hospital at Camp Holloway outside Pleiku, a former French site with an airfield. I was strapped to a bed, so I couldn't roll over, with many IVs and my arm extended on a bracket arrangement bolted to the bed. The set-up kept me elevated and stable. The hospital/airfield complex was attacked that night by the NVA, and in the space of five minutes or so two 122 mm rockets exploded in the hospital wing. Many aircraft were destroyed, and we had small-arms fire perforating the tin sides of the hospital, though all up high. There was lots of commotion as the place was overflowing with Tet casualties and Slicks coming in continuously. But that's another story.

ORRIN LEONARD DYER JR

CWO - W2 - Army – Reserve

38 years old, Married, Caucasian, Male

Born Jul 1, 1929

From Rumney, New Hampshire

Length of service 18 years.

His tour of duty began on Jun 16, 1967

Casualty Feb 3, 1968

In Kon Tum, South Vietnam

Hostile, helicopter – Pilot

Air loss, Crash on land

Body was recovered

Religion Methodist

Panel 37E -- Line 6

CWO Orrin Dyer:
KIA on February 3, 1968
in Đắk Tô.

Lieutenant Larry Skoglund:
Larry was with CWO
Dyer on February 3, 1968.

Special Forces Camp at Ben Het: Hell on Earth.

The 105/106 mm recoilless rifle: lightweight and mobile.

Armored Personal Carrier (APC): We rode in this for over two hours en route to the Leper Village.

The OH-23G Raven was a versatile and reliable helicopter,
used mostly in Vietnam for forward artillery observation
and scouting. The author experienced more close calls
on the OH-23G than he did when flying on the gunships.

B-52: The ground would shake for miles during
a B-52 bombardment often referred to as "Arc Light."
The B-52 made 26 bombing missions at Dak To in November 1967.

Đắk Tô, where there was never
a dull moment.

Firebase 14, west of Kon Tum
where the author was wounded at the right circle
and dragged while under fire by Lt. Rich to the circle
on the left on April 4th 1968.

The 8" Howitzer was accurate up to 25 miles and was the infantry soldier's best friend.

DEPARTMENT OF THE ARMY
HEADQUARTERS
FIRST US ARMY SUPPORT ELEMENT
FORT GEORGE G. MEADE, MARYLAND 20755

13 June 1969

Mr. Paul G. Mittelstaedt
17 Valiant Drive
Rochester, New York

Dear Mr. Mittelstaedt:

Enclosed is the Army Commendation Medal for Heroism awarded
to you for heroism while serving in the Republic of Viet Nam.

It is a pleasure to have had you as a member of my command.
I regret that this award was not received sufficiently in advance
to have made a formal presentation while you were still on
active duty.

Please accept my belated congratulations on behalf of the United
States Army for your bravery and devotion to duty against a
hostile force.

Sincerely,

EUGENE J. WHITE
Colonel, Armor
Commanding

f

The Wall

 Ceremony for those 173rd
Airborne troopers
KIA on Hill 875,
November 1967.

Anti-War Protest

**The Bell UH 1B and C were
primarily gunships equipped with 7.62 mm
mini-guns, 2.75" rockets and two
M60 equipped door gunners.**

B 40 Rocket

**The NVA/VC B-40 rocket was very
effective and deadly.**

h

ONCE A BOY

Chapter 10

THE RAT

Television brought the brutality of war into the comfort of the living room. Vietnam was lost in the living rooms of America, not on the battlefields of Vietnam. Marshall McLuhan

≈≈≈

It's been three days since CWO Orrin Dyer was KIA here at Dak To. I'm still here and carrying out my duties. Lt. Rich is now the DIVARTY pilot I have been assigned to. Lt. Rich and I will have many experiences together here at Dak To and Kon Tum over the next two months. He's a Louisiana boy, only a few years older than I, who likes having me and my M60 on board with him on fire missions. He'll request my attendance when the situation calls for it. He knew CWO Dyer well and was deeply saddened by his loss.

My schedule was pretty simple: I go to the airfield; do the daily inspection, including checking the rotor head safety wires, checking all fluids; start the OH-23; check the magnetos; run the rpms to a certain level; and apply the collective stick and hover the craft to make sure all systems are in good working condition. My routine is concluded when I sign off in the green log book, light up a smoke and watch as supply transports make their daily deliveries of troops and supplies.

Security was at a heightened level as the Tet Offensive was winding down, but it was far from over. The daily mortar and rocket strike were unpredictable, but you could count on a few of the projectiles anytime day or night. The rumors of a ground assault put us on high alert, and leaving yourself vulnerable was the order of the day, every day.

When I left 4th Aviation's gunships in January, I figured my chances of returning home had increased tenfold. The next two months would, however, prove me wrong. A multitude of opportunities to put myself in harm's way would materialize primarily because of my eagerness to be involved! Around February 9th, I made my way to the airfield to prepare the OH-23 Raven for that day's adventure. I finished my inspection and kicked back to admire the beautiful morning. The day was quiet, still and crystal clear. Off in the distance I could see a C-130 Hercules aircraft making its final approach, landing gear down, full flaps and about to touch down. That's just when off in the distance, an all too familiar sound interrupted my attention. It was an all too familiar thumping sound of an NVA mortar round leaving its tube en route to take out the incoming aircraft. In a matter of a few seconds a multitude of thumps and the whooshing sounds of 122 mm rockets broke the silence that only a few minutes ago I was enjoying so much.

There are three places you don't want to be when mortars and rockets are raining down. One is the airfield, second is the ammo dump, and third is the fuel bladders. All three of those are within eyesight, and running between them to get back to the safety of our bunker at this point was not an option. The C-130 was now at the end of the airstrip, and with no hesitation it quickly made a U-turn. Under full throttle the pilot set his course to get the Hell out here. All four of the C-130's propeller-driven engines were at full power when it flew by me. I vividly recall how it sounded, but trying to express that sound on paper is impossible. Three, maybe four mortar rounds impacted about two hundred yards to the west of me, followed by another, then another. I was in between the proverbial rock and a hard place. The deafening explosions sent rocks and dirt flying high in the air. I couldn't run toward our safe bunker as the explosions were in a direct line blocking my escape.

I am stuck on this airfield with nowhere to hide. The NVA would typically launch a mortar or rocket, and using that one round as a guide, adjust up or down and walk additional rounds to their intended target, which today appeared to be the C-130 that had just landed but was now gone. Directly behind me were the aviation fuel bladders protected by sandbags stacked a few feet high, and now that the C-130 had made its escape, it appeared by the direction of the incoming rounds that other aircraft and the fuel bladders were now their second choice. My moments of being a spectator came to an abrupt end when I dove behind a sandbag wall sandwiched with steel runway material standing on end. The time elapsed between the first explosion and my cowering was probably a mere two, maybe three minutes. Things happen fast here and you better be quick. I wrapped my arms around my helmet-less head and heard and felt the explosions get louder and closer. One particular explosion sounded different, as later I discovered a parked Huey took a direct hit and exploded, igniting fuel and munitions on board.

Three rounds impacted on my side of the wall. One hit so close I felt my body lift off the ground. My ears rang like a church bell, and then I felt this warm liquid on my face. I raised my arm and saw that the liquid was blood—my blood. I frantically felt my head, desperately trying to find the origin of the red liquid. I felt no pain other than a numbness from the close explosion only moments before. Our artillery was now engaged, firing dozens of Howitzer rounds at point-blank range of the mountains west of us. The area directly to the east of the airstrip erupted as the NVA rockets, and mortars were now coming from that direction. I don't know how far away the F-4 Phantom jets were stationed, but they were here in a hurry. First Air Cav helicopter gunships were airborne and they were now in the mix.

The jets streaked across the sky flying directly over me on their way to deposit the 750 lb bombs on the rocket ridge. Their 6-barrel 20 mm rotating guns were firing as they passed overhead, and their shell casings fell like rain. It didn't take long for the artillery rounds and the F-4's ordnance to bring the NVA's attack to an abrupt halt. *Silence has never been so golden,* I thought.

I waited until I had assured myself that the incoming rounds had stopped. I slowly stood up and was about to look where my blood was coming from when a young three-stripe Sergeant infantry soldier walked up to me, asked if I was OK and then made some comment about me not having a helmet or flak jacket on. A little dazed, I told him I was bleeding somewhere. He looked me over, raised my right arm to find embedded in my wrist a piece of metal the size of a quarter.

The Sergeant had a Jeep. "C'mon" he said. "I'll give you a lift to the aid station." I guess the blood that was running down my cheek was from that piece in my wrist, which was better than being stuck in my head. At the aid station about fifteen guys, some on stretchers, some not, were in line waiting for a medic to attend to their wounds. The stretchers obviously went first and were hurried into the MASH unit. About a half hour after my arrival, a medic came over, looked at my measly wound and pulled the metal piece from my wrist. He filled out a form, handed it to me and said, "Give this to your First Sergeant and he'll put you in for a purple. As I looked around, I saw guys with some pretty nasty wounds. I was embarrassed to think I would get a Purple Heart for this little piece a metal, and so I graciously declined.

"Hey, it's up to you, soldier," the young medic replied. My little pathetic wrist wound was bandaged and I was released.

I walked back to the airfield to see if our OH-23 had sustained any damage. The Huey that was hit earlier and covered in white-fire foam was only fifty feet or so from our revetment. Mortar craters were everywhere. It looked like a moonscape. There were several larger craters that were credited to 122 mm rockets. I remember hearing that all too familiar whoosh that the 122s make as they seek out their intended targets. I heard later that over forty mortars and rockets landed inside the perimeter. An Army engineer unit was already repairing the damaged runway and roads leading to it.

Lt. Rich was doing a walk around looking for damage on our OH-23 when I arrived. "Where you been?" he asked. I raised my right hand and showed him my bandage. "It's just a scratch," I said, downplaying the incident. We couldn't find any visible damage, so Lt. Rich fired up the OH-23, hovered it in place, set it down and together we walked up the flight line in order to see if we could be of any assistance. Several helicopters were damaged but nothing like the Huey that took a direct hit. Lt. Rich headed for the operations center while I made my way back to our bunker. The area mess tent took a hit, so breakfast was out of the question. A can of C-rations and a Coke would have to do.

Although not as vigorous as Tet, enemy activity was enough to keep us on our toes and on high alert. I never went to the airfield again without my helmet, flak jacket and weapon. The constant threat of enemy contact was ever present. An additional 4th Infantry Division unit was in camp to secure our perimeter from a ground assault that never came but could have.

A few of these "grunts" would stop by and use the shower we had built. I would trade showers for just about anything: C-rations, captured enemy weapons, pith helmets and flags. The best one was a pizza. The head cook at the officers' mess used to be a chef in New York City. He would drop off homemade jelly donuts and other baked goods. As I mentioned earlier, I rarely ate at a mess tent.

Lt. Rich informed me that Capt. Broyer would be spending two nights with us. "Broyer is deathly afraid of rats," Lt. Rich said. Rats made visits each night looking for food. In the dirt wall about eye level, we had cut a ledge four inches wide to set candles and other stuff on. It was also the rats' super-highway. I couldn't shoot them with real bullets, so I would remove the bullet and pack the shell casing with soap or wax and blast them. It wouldn't kill them, but they would squeal and run out of our bunker. I had a blank suppressor for my M16 that allowed me to produce enough back pressure and fire three or four rounds before the wax or soap would melt from the burning gunpowder. Capt. Broyer arrived late that day and requested the cot nearest the door, and we knew why. I was reading a letter from home, Lt. Rich was reading a book, and Capt. Broyer was writing a letter when I noticed the beady little red eyes of a very large rat entering the bunker. Broyer didn't see it, but Lt. Rich and I did. Lt. Rich looked at me with a childish grin as I picked up my M16, took the safety off and screamed "rats" followed by three rapid fire M16 rounds. Broyer screamed like a child. His letter went one direction, his pencil the other, and in an Olympic athlete's effort he beat the rat out of the bunker. Lt. Rich and I were laughing hysterically at Broyer's foot race with the rat. I felt bad for the rat finishing second.

We anxiously awaited Broyer's return. He returned a few minutes later and tore in to us for this prank and for firing my weapon inside the bunker. Lt. Rich tried desperately to keep a straight face while he explained they weren't real bullets. Those were the last words spoken that night. Actually Capt. Broyer only stayed one night. *I wonder why.* Capt. Broyer never, not once, ever spoke to me again. Forty-five years later when I found Lt. Rich, he couldn't wait to tell me that he had only a few days earlier told someone the "rat" story. We laughed out loud recalling the foot race between Broyer and the rat. More on that conversation later with Lt. Rich.

Capt. Hagen flew in and stayed three nights while Lt. Rich went to Kon Tum to ferry a high-ranking officer around to a couple of forward firebases. I was surprised to hear that Capt. Hagen was a career soldier. He was somewhat sophisticated, had a perfect haircut and a handlebar mustache that set the standard for handlebar mustaches. He was due to return to the States soon and this was his last Dak To visit. He was always reading a book and listening to classical music. He was religious and wanted nothing to do with an M60 hanging from his helicopter door. His reasoning was simple. First, if you shoot at someone, they tend to shoot back. Secondly, I don't want to be responsible for your safety. He carried his Philco record player with him wherever he went and loved jazz and classical music.

Late at night in the bunker we would eventually grow tired of reading or writing, and we would talk until one of us fell asleep. He wasn't like the others at all. I don't recall how old he was, but my guess was late thirties, maybe. He would take off in the morning, be gone for a while and return early to mid-afternoon. I never flew with

Hagen, and the other pilots never spoke about him like they did each other. Odd chemistry, I guess.

Lt. Rich returned just before dark last night, noting that being a taxi driver was not what he had signed up for. I readied Capt. Hagen's aircraft as he was heading back to Enari to start his journey home. I noticed that he didn't have his Philco with him.

"Sir, your record player! Should I fetch it for you?"

"Not necessary," Capt. Hagen replied. "It was passed down to me. The Philco is now yours."

"Thank you, Capt. Hagen." In my mind's eye I can still see him lift off and give me a kind of a wave goodbye.

Lt. Rich came to the airfield while I was doing his daily inspection. "Go grab your things, we have a project," he said. "A Bird Dog (a fixed wing, single-engine Cessna) was shot down near Ben Het. They rescued the pilot, but the aircraft is pretty much intact, and it needs to be destroyed before the NVA get the radios and maps that were left behind."

"OK, I'll be right back," I said, as I double-timed back to our bunker for the tools of my trade. When I returned, I found Lt. Rich waiting on the runway. I hooked the M60's bungee cord to the door frame, put my helmet on, buckled up, and off we went.

The Lieutenant said, "I need you to put your tracer rounds into the aircraft with hopes of igniting the fuel tank."

"What if that doesn't work?" I asked.

His reply was what I had anticipated. "We'll call in artillery rounds. We'll try and save the taxpayers a couple of bucks. Have you ever called in an artillery strike?" he asked me. "No, never," I said. The fifteen-minute flight seemed a lot longer as I was excited about this mission. I spotted the Cessna first and it seemed to be in pretty good shape. We stayed a distance away and at altitude just in case unfriendlies were nearby. Lt. Rich held us as steady as he could as I started with short-bursts until I got the hang of the altitude and distance. My tracers found their mark, and after a few bursts—maybe 200 rounds fired—there was no sign of a fire. It could be that the fuel had already drained from the initial crash.

"OK," Lt. Rich said, "we're going to call in a fire mission. I'll give you the coordinates and call signs and coaching when needed." If you recall, I struggled with map reading. It went something like this:

"Red Dog base, this is Red Leg 6 Fire mission. Over."

"Red Dog base, Red Leg 6 location 1-2-3-4. Over." (the first 4 digits of the map coordinates)

"Red Dog base, Red Leg 6 location 6-7-8-niner. Over." (the last 4 digits of the map coordinates.)

"Red Dog base, Red Leg 6, 1 smoke."

It took 20 seconds or so, and Red Base gave us a compass reading, so we knew what direction the round was coming from. A division artillery unit at Ben Het is where the fire mission would originate.

"Red Leg 6, Red Dog base, round out!"

In a matter of seconds, the round exploded about 200 meters past our intended target.

"Red Dog base, Red Leg 6, drop 200 meters. Red Leg 6, round out."

This round fell short of our target by 50 meters. Lt. Rich keyed up for me alone and said, "Tell them plus 50 and fire for effect."

I keyed my mike and said, "Red Dog Base, Red Leg 6. Plus 50 and fire for effect." Maybe 15-20 seconds later, "Red Leg 6, Red Dog base, rounds out."

Unbelievable! About two seconds later the entire battery of 155 mm howitzers at Ben Het sent a salvo of rounds—eight, maybe ten rounds, maybe more on target. A secondary explosion signaled that the Cessna was no longer with us, but there was more to come. Lt. Rich and I saw it at the same time—muzzle flashes. We were being shot at. At the elevation we were at, an AK-47 round would pretty much be out of gas by the time it got to us. Lt. Rich quickly moved the OH-23 to a safe distance, keyed his radio and said,

"Red Dog Base, this is Red Leg 6. Enemy combatants on target. Repeat fire mission times 2. Do you copy? Over."

"Red Leg 6, Red Dog Base times 2, rounds out."

The landscape below went through a dramatic overhaul as round after round poured into the area. I emptied my M60 ammo box at the location of the muzzle flash's earlier location while another moonscape courtesy of the US Army artillery was underway. Lt. Rich surmised that we could do no more there, so he turned the OH-23 south and at a safe altitude and set sail for Dak To airfield. Ben Het was closer if fuel was an issue, but as I said earlier, Ben Het is 'bad ass' and not the place to stop and fill up. Passing us going in the opposite direction were four helicopter gunships most likely on their way to where we just left.

My adrenaline was flowing like never before. We landed, unbuckled and walked around the aircraft looking for any damage. My face was hurting from ear to ear due to the grin I was wearing. Lt. Rich looked at me and gently shook his head, acknowledging my excitement over what just took place. "That was pretty cool," I said. I wouldn't even think of doing that again if there were friendly forces nearby. What a responsibility to call in deadly artillery when our ground troops are nearby. Friendly fire incidents are impossible to accurately count, but it is estimated that a few thousand died at the hands of their own troops. Lt. Rich didn't say "good job" or offer any high fives for my first effort, but I figured if he let me do it again that it would be a good sign.

Dak To was to be my home until the middle of March. Two or three pilots would share the bunker with me, but I didn't fly much as the pilots after Lt. Rich didn't have that adventurous nature that Lt. Rich and I had. I have become rather fond of this place. I have my Philco, plenty of Coke, Jack Daniels, and my new Super 8 movie camera that Mom bought me for my early birthday present. The thought of going back to base camp and routine formations, details and all the other nonsense is probably why I like it here so much. I'll have to shave as well. I hate shaving! All toll, I have spent a larger portion of my tour here. (Tour? Sounds like a cruise, doesn't it?) I remember everything about Dak To—the smell, the sounds, the mountains. I would love to go back and stand on the very spot where the bunker was and where the airfield once lay.

I think a lot about Dak To. CWO Dyer, the net, the rat and other events that contributed to the resume of a twenty-year-old boy's life story.

Chapter 11

SMOKE RINGS

We went to war because our country called us. It was our heritage, our duty, our honor, our love of country, or I really wasn't doing anything else at the time.

≈≈≈

In early March Lt. Rich came back and informed me that he and I would be rotating back to Camp Enari in a few days. He must have noticed my disappointment and quickly added that he and another pilot would soon be assigned to a Mechanized Infantry Unit near Kon Tum.

"Two crew chiefs would be needed . . . any interest?" asked Lt. Rich.

I couldn't have answered any quicker. "Absolutely, count me in."

"We still have some work to do here, however," said the Lieutenant. "We have a large bag of mail that needs to get up to Ben Het. They haven't gotten mail for over a week." Ben Het? To this day those two words spike my blood pressure. I've landed there maybe two or three times, and each time we had to get out in a hurry. Ben Het was a 5th Special Forces (Green Beret) base northwest of Dak To. The camp was notable for being the site of a tank battle between the U.S. Army and NVA/PAVN in March 1969. May and June saw some of the fiercest fighting of the Vietnam War. This camp monitored enemy movement near the tri-borders of Laos, Cambodia and Vietnam and seemed to be a hotbed for enemy activity.

Lt. Rich was precise in what he said to me as we approached the runway. "When we land, someone will meet us at the center of the runway. Unbuckle the bag, give it to him and we're out of there." He couldn't have been any clearer. As we approached, I saw a tall, slim soldier clad in neatly pressed camouflaged fatigues, Army green T-shirt, flak jacket and helmet. He was waving his arms signaling that he was the guy we were looking for. Lt. Rich set the 23 down gently, and then I unbuckled, jumped out, grabbed the mail bag and hauled it over to the awaiting soldier.

"Hey man, thanks. We really appreciate it," he said.

"You're welcome," I replied.

"Where you from?" the soldier asked. "Rochester, New York," I said in a hurry.

"I've been there . . . it's near Buffalo, right?

"Yeah," I said as I turned away.

"How many days you got left?" he asked. Man, this guy wants to chat and we want out of here.

"Hey bud, we really gotta go," I said, and as I looked at Lt. Rich and got the evil eye, I gave the guy a half of a wave goodbye, climbed aboard, and before I was buckled in we were lifting off. We couldn't have been more than twenty feet off the ground when an explosion near the middle of the camp sent dirt and debris high in the air followed by yet another and another explosion. This place was under attack! Lt. Rich put the pedal to the metal, and we were up and away and cleared the camp and the danger of the explosions.

We moved a little south of the camp and watched as Lt. Rich communicated with someone there, apparently asking if we were needed to call in enemy coordinates. Lt. Rich pointed our nose back toward the camp, and then smoke rings appeared just north of their wire about half a mile or so at just inside the tree line. Lt. Rich shouted, "Recoilless rifle." Recoilless rifles on a calm day would produce a smoke ring when fired. The NVA forces were firing rounds as quickly as they could reload. "Put your ' 60 on them," he said to me as we moved closer. I had about 800 rounds in the box, and I walked those tracer rounds toward the enemy rifle. Somewhere around 400 rounds an explosion took place at the rifle's location. Another explosion at the same spot, then another. I kept firing until I was empty. As cool and calm as Lt. Rich could be the firing came to an end when he shouted, "God dammit, you got 'em. That's a secondary explosion; you touched off their fucking rounds." I tried to be cool and collected for about two seconds and then I let out a "Yeeeaaah!" Lt. Rich slapped my knee and was ecstatic with expletives that I never heard him utter before. Whoever he was communicating with down below shouted back, "Nice shooting, you guys. Man, that was frigging incredible. Thank you, guys, we owe you one." Ben Het had its own artillery unit of 105- and 155-mm Howitzers and sent round after round into the same area. As we moved away, I continued to watch the exchange, thinking Dak To was bad, but this place is crazy. I never heard that day or any day after if that exchange lasted any period of time or if any casualties were a result.

Lt. Rich turned the 23 back south and we headed to Dak To. We landed, did the normal routine inspection, and then Lt. Rich calls me over to his side of the ship and points at three bullet holes on the underside of the skids and motor mount area. I was pumped. The bullets passed through everything cleanly with no damage other than to the sheet metal.

"A flesh wound," Lt. Rich said. "Come with me." He was more excited than I was. I had never been to the operations hooch with any of the pilots before, but he wanted to show the others the sharpshooter who took out the recoilless rifle. "Great job," "nice shot," "good shooting" were but a few of the compliments in addition to back slaps, handshakes and enough accolades to last a lifetime. Well, a few Jack Daniels and a little Coca Cola later and I was asleep in the bunker with Lt. Rich and probably a rat or two.

Two days later Lt. Rich and I flew back to Camp Enari much to my dismay to get ready for our next duty in Kon Tum. All the pilots, except Broyer (Rat), paid me compliments over the Ben Het caper.

The other crew chiefs never said a word. If you recall, the other crew chiefs thought I was setting a precedent by arming and flying with the pilots and that they would be expected do the same. Well, too bad! I was on cloud nine and they weren't invited.

Base camp sucks. It took our flight commander, Capt. Bacon, to instruct our company commander, Capt. Asbury, to strike my name from any and all detail lists. Capt. Bacon (Skip) was pretty impressed with the taking out the recoilless rifle and told Capt. Asbury that I was preparing for deployment to Kon Tum and was busy preparing supplies to be trucked there. We had no bunker there, so we went to supply and had a 15 by 15 tent, 5 cots, sleeping bags, lanterns and other supplies readied to truck there. Drew Taylor from Buffalo was the other crew chief assigned to go. I don't recall the other pilot's name for this adventure, but I think his name was Warrant Officer Williams. He was a newbie and this was his first forward adventure. I had my five-ton driver's license from my bus driving days at Ft. Rucker and Ft. Wolters, so Drew and I would drive the truck to Kon Tum. I had driven on convoys before and didn't mind. There was, however, always the threat of mines and ambush, so we decided to wait and join a large convoy. Safety in numbers always seemed to be a good bet.

≈≈≈

Beautiful day for a drive, I thought. It was sunny and warm, and I was anxious to get out of Dodge. We drove to Pleiku, which was normally an hour or more. We would hook up with the convoy at Camp Holloway at 0600 hours (we do everything at 0600 hours), and from there it was about thirty miles, but with checkpoints and mine sweeping we expected to be on the road a couple of hours or more, usually more.

Hurry-up in wait was the norm in the Army and wait we did. It was almost 1200 hours before we started. We found out later that a sniffer detected enemy combatants near Highway 14 about eight miles from our destination. A sniffer was usually attached to a Huey H

Model with long poles protruding out the front with an attached device that could detect scents such as urine and body odor of humans. I saw one of these at Dak To last November. It got quite a workout there.

We finally arrived about 1800 hours. Lt. Rich was waiting there and wondering why it took 12 hours to drive 50 miles.

I said, "We stopped along the way, caught a movie and a couple of Piña Coladas at the beach," followed by a chuckle. He didn't seem to appreciate the humor, and if he did, he wasn't about to laugh anyway.

Someone picked out a spot for our tent. We dragged the tent off the truck and started to level the ground with these tiny little shovels and a makeshift rake that we found nearby. We got some help from some supply people with stakes and poles to get our tent in the air. The next day we were filling sandbags to put around the tent when someone remarked about a terrible odor that worsened as the sun warmed the ground. *It had to be something in the ground,* I thought.

An Army engineer was walking by and asked, "Why did you pick that place for a tent?

The supply Sergeant that was helping us asked, "What's wrong with this place?"

The Army engineer answered, "Well, your tent is on top of a mass grave of NVA soldiers." Everyone immediately stopped what they were doing and listened to the engineer's explanation.

"There's over a hundred enemy soldiers under your feet." I bulldozed that hole myself last November. You might want to move your tent." We stood there with blank expressions, and then someone asked, "Got any suggestions?"

"Yeah," the engineer said, "come with me." The new location looked good enough, but it's now late afternoon so we had two choices: 1) sleep on top of the grave, or 2) bum a bunk from someone who has available space. Needless to say, we chose the second option.

Lt. Rich and I flew each day. We'd go up with an experienced, young Lieutenant from Indiana and really didn't have any enemy contact as these were mapping missions. They were boring, to say the least. The NVA were amazing as they would move large numbers of soldiers all over the place without being detected. One of our flights took us to a remote firebase named Mary Lou (Firebase 14), which would play the biggest part of my tour in about three weeks. Of course, I didn't know that then.

Firebase 14 was a cleared hill about the size of a Walmart. There was no enemy activity the day we were there, but it got its share of enemy mortars and rockets. After several days, Lt. Rich told me we were no longer needed here and that he and I would be going back to base camp and return if needed. Drew Taylor and WO Williams would stay at Kon Tum for the time being. Drew offered to go back instead of me, but Lt. Rich nixed that in a hurry. While flying back to base camp Lt. Rich shared with me that we'd be back at Kon Tum soon enough as enemy supply buildup had increased on the trail (Ho Chi Minh), and that was always a good indication that they were planning an offensive.

I have about 120 days remaining on my tour. If I extend my tour here for six months, I can get an "early out" from my three-year enlistment. I think I've been pretty lucky so far and pushing my luck here is not a good idea. One can only dodge so many bullets.

Chapter 12

NUMBER 7

I was in the operations hooch retrieving updated maps for Lt. Rich. In the corner sat a hand-cuffed NVA Officer who they were preparing to fly back to the Camp Holloway. I couldn't help but hear him speaking perfect English. An Infantry Officer that was interrogating him asked him about his English. "I studied in your country at the University of Indiana," *he said apologetically. The Infantry asked why he came back here. The NVA officer's reply was direct and heartfelt:* "You invaded my country."

≈≈≈

Idle time in the military far outweighs actual time spent engaged with the enemy. In previous wars the combat soldier was engaged less than forty days out of a four-year enlistment. The American combat soldier in Vietnam was engaged over 240 days a year. I get bored very easily and I must have something to do. Sitting around the hooch playing cards or singing Peter, Paul & Mary songs with a guitar player from Brooklyn was not for me.

Most of the pilots knew I were game for just about anything. They would invite me to fly with them on artillery missions, reconnaissance and taxi service for an officer of rank. My gunship days gave me confidence in the operation of the M60 machine gun that hung from the door frame by a bungee cord.

The pilots felt safer with me riding shotgun for a couple of reasons. First, I had attended helicopter flight school in Mineral Wells, Texas. I had soloed in a similar helicopter before I dropped out for medical reasons. If something happened to the pilot, I guess they figured I'd get them back safely. Second, I had the M60 machine gun, knew how to use it and would, if necessary, do just that.

My favorite pilot—Lt. Rich—would often ask me to accompany him on many occasions, and I never refused. Looking back, I wish that I had passed on this one. It was March 1968. Enemy activity was still high in the Central Highlands. Although we defeated the VC and NVA one month earlier during the Tet Offensive, they were still wreaking havoc. Dealing injuries and death to our forces is what they do best, and there was no such thing as taking a break or a day off. Every day was a Monday.

About 0800 hours Lt. Rich stuck his head through the hooch door, spotted me, and wondered why I wasn't at the airfield yet. I replied that I wasn't aware I was going anywhere, but I do now. My stuff was always ready to go. So, I grabbed all the tools of my trade and made my way to the airfield.

On arrival I saw that Lt. Rich had already done his pre-flight and was buckled in and ready to go. I hooked my M60 to the bungee cord, buckled up and signaled that I was ready. I keyed the microphone and inquired on what our destination was. "Plei Mrong," he said. It was cooler this morning than most, creating some ground fog. As we gained altitude the light ground fog disappeared and we were on our way. We would be picking up a FAC (Forward Air Controller) at the Plei Mrong Special Forces Camp northwest of Pleiku about halfway to Kon Tum. Today's mission was to flush out, no kill, a reported enemy company that was spotted by an LRRP team just a few kilometers from the Laotian border. Although Lt. Rich was capable calling in artillery, most ground troops preferred their FO's (Forward Observers) working with their own FAC's (Forward Air Controllers) familiar with the terrain and each other.

As we approached the Special Forces Camp, I saw this young, baby faced, Second Lieutenant standing near the chopper landing pad marked with a big X. This young, little boy was our FAC. I don't think he even shaves yet, I thought. He was tiny, baby faced and couldn't weigh any more than one of my legs.

Listening to the Lt. Rich and the 2nd Lt. Baby Face, I learned that an NVA company of about 200 plus soldiers was cornered in a valley west of Plei Mrong. The objective was simple. Unleash a barrage of 155mm Howitzers from a nearby firebase, driving what's left of them north and into the waiting 4th Division Infantry soldiers blocking their escape. Second Lt. Baby Face directed Lt. Rich to a location that would be out of the way of incoming rounds. The ground fog here had not lifted yet when Lt. Baby Face called in the target co-ordinates. The 105 and 155mm Howitzers fired salvo after salvo into the distant valley below. Strange how some things stick in your memory. As the artillery rounds passed through the fog there was this corkscrew swirling movement as the fog parted ways to let the artillery rounds in. We were more amazed with the projectiles swirling through fog than what their objective was. Anyway, enough of that.

Second Lieutenant Baby Face signed off with his FO and the artillery unit. His mission was complete, and with that we would drop him off where we had picked him up and head back to our airfield. As we approached the firebase landing pad, I noticed a couple of soldiers waiting for us. They held their Green Berets close to their heads with one hand so as not to lose them with our blade wash. Lt. Rich keyed his microphone and said "What do suppose they want? I guess we'd find out soon enough, eh?"

One of the two soldiers waiting for us was a Maj. Toms. The other soldier was a Sgt. Simms. These guys had perfect fitting camo fatigues. The Major looked like he was fresh out of a movie. Maj. Toms signaled Lt. Rich to shut down our ride. The rotor blades came to a stop. It didn't take a rocket scientist to figure out that we weren't done here and they had something else for us to do.

While Lt. Rich was talking to the very large and well-fit Green Beret, Maj. Sgt. Simms approached me, handed me the six-foot pole with make shift hook on the end, looked in the direction of Lt. Rich and with Maj. Toms looking on gave us these instructions. Our men caught seven or eight NVA in the open about two kilometers from here.

Maj. Toms interrupted by saying, "We need you to go there, search the bodies for maps or anything that may disclose operations." Sgt. Simms nodded at the pole. "You'll use this to roll over the bodies. Lie on the ground, hook, roll and cover for about thirty seconds in case they were booby trapped. Bring anything you find back here."

As Sgt. Simms and Maj. Toms walked away, I looked at Lt. Rich and said: "Are you kidding me? We're not trained for this." Lt. Rich, knowing full well he couldn't disobey an order from a Major, got in, buckled up and started the Lycoming upright six-cylinder engine. I stood motionless for a few moments wondering what I was supposed to do. *What if there are other NVA lying in wait with thoughts of taking revenge for their loss?*

I was surprised to see 2nd Lt. Baby Face climb back in and buckle up. It must have been suggested by Maj. Tom for him to ride along. I secured the pole with the makeshift hook on the skids, buckled up and gave Lt. Rich the thumbs up that I was ready to depart.

Lt. Rich opened the throttle, pulled the collective stick up, and we made another smooth take off. We headed to the given coordinates through the light haze still present. This place had an unusual smell to it. There always seemed to be something burning wherever we go. Never gave that much thought until today. *Maybe enemy bodies? Something smells.*

It took all of five minutes to get there. As we approached the open field adjacent to a rice paddy, I could see the bodies of the enemy soldiers that I was going search. A few hours ago, they would have loved to kill me. "Not today," I said to myself.

There were seven of them. Almost in a circle, except one who was maybe twenty-five or thirty feet away. Their guns were gone but otherwise they looked dead. Seven more families ruined!

I unbuckled, grabbed the pole with makeshift hook and started toward the deceased. I soon realized I was alone. Lt. Rich stayed in the chopper for good reason. If something went afoul and we needed to get out there he was ready. On the other hand, 2nd Lt. Baby Face made no attempt to follow me.

I'm twenty-years old from Rochester, New York. I'm a Yankee fan, I love Mom's apple pie, I love my brothers and sisters, I go to church and someday I want a fast car. *What on earth am I doing here? I have no experience in this exercise that has been thrust upon me. I want to get out of here, so I better search these bodies. Where do I start?* I figured out pretty quickly about the pole with the makeshift hook. I laid down in a prone position, hooked the clothing of the dead man, rolled him over, and waited about thirty seconds. If there is no explosion, I would stand up with plenty of hesitation and start my search for documents. I would not recommend taking the assignment of searching dead bodies if the job was ever offered to you. Trust me on this one.

If I'd eaten a big breakfast that morning it would be somewhere down my pant leg by now. This moment terrified me. It wasn't the first time I was scared, but it was the most I've ever been. I mean ever! My heart rate had to be off the charts. I went the aviation route so this kind of stuff wouldn't happen, but here I am.

There wasn't much of anything in the pockets of the first three that I checked. A little money, letters, notes and rice balls. The fourth one had something that is burned into that ironclad mind's eye of mine. It was a photograph, and in that photograph was a young man, a woman, and a child. Oh my God! This guy's family. What made it worse was a black and white mutt, the family dog, man's best friend right in the middle. Just another reminder that these were people with friends, families and pets.

I looked back at my ride out of here, and Lt. Rich and 2nd Lt. Baby Face seemed to be disinterested in what I was doing. I kept waiting for 2nd Lt. Baby Face to get out and help me, but that wasn't happening. Hell, I'm an enlisted soldier; he's an officer. I'm cheap labor.

The fifth and sixth soldier had nothing worth retrieving. Number 7, the one that was thirty feet away was the larger one of the fallen soldiers. I was tempted to call it quits while I was ahead but convinced myself to finish the job. I figured these guys must have been dead for a few hours as they seemed a little stiff. I got into my now accustomed prone position and set my makeshift hook on a piece of clothing of number 7 and proceeded to roll him over. My heart stopped when I realized this guy was not as rigid as the others. Actually, he wasn't even slightly stiff. I waited longer than the thirty seconds before I rose to my feet. I tried to get the attention of Lt. Rich, but he seemed preoccupied with maps.

I wasn't about to search this guy. I didn't care if he had the cure for cancer in his pocket. As I looked at him his eyes seemed moist, unlike the others which were glazed over. His lips were moist, not like the others that appeared to be purple. I didn't happen to have a brain surgeon available to tell me that this guy was still alive. I stood there staring at him for what seemed like an eternity trying to decide on what to do next. He had several bullet holes in his clothing and blood . . . fresh blood.

I am now quivering, no shaking! I look to the helicopter. I waved, shrugged my shoulders, pointed to number 7 and gave the outstretched arms signal. What should I do? Lt. Rich pointed at his watch and gave me a hurry-up gesture.

This twenty-year-old Henrietta, New York boy, away from home for the first time, was faced with the decision of a lifetime. Our helicopter seats three. All seats taken. He'll die sooner or later. As I stared at number 7 my mind started playing tricks on me. I think I saw his moist lips move. Maybe they did, maybe they didn't. Was he trying to talk?

For years I justified what I was about to do. I had only my .38 caliber Smith and Wesson pistol with me. I needed to do this quickly, otherwise I could talk myself out of it. I drew my pistol and ended his life with a bullet to his forehead. My heart rate at that very moment

102

had to be 150 beats a minute, about what it's beating right now as I re-live this event.

I returned to the aircraft, attached the pole with the makeshift hook to the skids, handed over the papers that I collected to 2nd Lt. Baby Face, buckled up and welcomed the liftoff from this nightmare. I glanced back at the circle of dead enemy and my eyes found number 7, clear as a bell, even today over fifty years later.

Lt. Rich keyed his microphone and asked if I was OK. I turned my head toward him and wanted to say something, but I couldn't. We never discussed it. With the helicopter running maybe he didn't hear the 38-caliber gun shot. I wasn't about to volunteer it anyway. I was happy that silence prevailed.

The flight back to 2nd Lt. Baby Face's location couldn't happen quick enough. I needed to get back home and down some alcohol. A lot of alcohol. That kind of adventure could easily fester a lasting relationship with a bottle of spirits. As we approached the landing spot, I noticed that Sgt. Simms and Maj. Toms were awaiting our arrival. We landed on the X. I gave Sgt. Simms his pole with a makeshift hookback and watched 2nd Lt. Baby Face hand over the found papers to Maj. Simms with a look of pride on his face as if he had risked his life to secure them. *So typical*, I thought.

Sitting on the ground next to our welcoming duo was what looked like a prisoner. His hands and feet were secured with army green rope. He was dressed like the circle of the seven unfortunate soldiers we recently left behind. He was a young NVA officer with the all too familiar markings of a recent interrogation.

Although I couldn't hear what Lt. Rich and the Maj. Toms were talking about, I kind of figured out that we were about to become a taxi. Lt. Rich, being the obedient soldier he was, walked toward me with a military policeman and this slightly built, worse-for-wear prisoner of war and attempted to sit him in one our three seats. I beat

Lt. Rich to the punch when I said, "He can't sit inside. We'll have to tie him to the skids. Do you have any more rope?"

With the help of the Military Policeman, we tied the prisoner securely to the skids and prepared to get out of this place. Our POW was not too thrilled about being hog-tied to the skids, but it was the only way he was going with us.

The young POW's hands were tied on the horizontal skid where I would often rest my foot. Funny thing, often in a golf cart I ride with my foot outside like that, and so I think of his experience. The overcast skies we saw earlier seemed to have moved away from us, and a threat of a storm that would keep us here any longer was gone. As we became airborne, I keyed my microphone and said to Lt. Rich, "Damn, is there anything else we can do for these guys?" Lt. Rich just shook his head and said, "We need this day to be over." I looked down at the young prisoner and wondered if he had anything to eat or drink. I had no food, but I did have a canteen of water. I opened it and moved it toward the prisoner's mouth. He looked at me with his dark eyes and now visible to me, for the first time, the bruises of interrogation. He quickly turned his head, refusing my offering.

We were about halfway into our twenty-five-minute flight home when Lt. Rich keyed his mike and asked, "How's our prisoner doing?"

"Oh, he's gone, I said.

"What?" the Lieutenant replied in disbelief.

"Just kidding," I said with a laugh. That was the first expressed emotion Lt. Rich displayed that day. I had hardly finished laughing when my foot was being attacked by the hog-tied hands of our prisoner. I quickly pulled my strayed foot from the skid. I guess I get the *He wanted to hurt me. I'm the enemy, the invader, the one who was delivering him to more interrogation and most likely a bruise or two on top of the ones he already had.*

Flying over Camp Holloway tells me we that are only a few minutes from home. A few minutes later the lights of Camp Enari become visible. As I'm thinking of that, my prisoner, well not really "my" prisoner, begins to shout in broken English. I didn't understand him at first but on about the third try I made out this: *I kill many GI. I will kill more! I kill you!* As Lt. Rich was hovering down to the X that marks the landing spot at the Military Police detention center, he keyed up and said, "Get our passenger ready." The passenger continued his rant on how he wanted to kill many GI's and me. I felt a little compassion for this POW knowing what was in store for him.

About ten feet off the landing pad my new worst enemy spit at me as I offered him a drink of water and went into a rage as he tried to untie his hands. "Enough is enough," I yelled. I cut the foot ties first and with one quick motion the front ties were severed and he was gone. He plunged all of ten feet. The MP's scurried to the landing, and as he was taken away his glare cut through the swirling dirt and sand created by the hovering craft's rotors.

Lt. Rich, while concentrating on another perfect hover and landing, looked at me and said, "Get ready to cut him loose."

"Too late," I said, "He's already gone." I pointed to the MP's walking him away. Through the opening in his flight helmet, I saw the raised eyebrow followed with a grin.

The short flight from the MP station to our airfield was short. A chill was in the air that I hadn't felt earlier. I think that maybe my mind was pretty occupied most of the day. I unbuckled, tied down the rotor, and with flight book filled out I was off to the hooch. Carrying all my gear seemed much lighter earlier today.

I entered the hooch as the evening set in. Most of the guys were writing letters or reading them. Bob Miles asked, "How'd it go out there today?"

"OK, I guess! Nothing unusual!

Chapter 13

EYE TO EYE

I do not believe that the men who served in uniform in Vietnam have been given the credit they deserve. It was a difficult war against an unorthodox enemy. - General William Westmoreland

≈≈≈

With over one hundred days remaining on my tour, I'm anxious to get to the double-digit fidget. I've been fortunate up to this point. I've had more than enough close calls, but I never wavered in my hopes to get home alive. The new day greeted me with as beautiful a morning as one could expect for being in a war zone. It was sunny, clear and rapidly warming up as the sun made its way over Signal Mountain. I had spent the last two months dodging rockets and mortars at Dak To and Kon Tum in the Central Highlands. I preferred forward outposts over base camps because I was in charge of me. Making sure our equipment was safe and operational was my duty, and although we endured daily rocket and mortar attacks, I felt most useful up there in the forward outposts.

The infamous Tet Offensive was pretty much over, but the NVA (North Vietnam) Regulars were not about to give up, and they seemed to be everywhere. It was only a few months ago, in November of 1967, at the battles for Hill 875, 861 and others when 376 young men died and another 1441 were wounded. Those events in Dak To and nearby Kon Tum will not be forgotten by anyone who served with the 4th Division, 173rd Airborne and others. I think of them often.

Our unit commander, Capt. Bacon, decided I needed a rest from all of the chaos, and so he ordered me back to our base at Camp Enari for a break. I shaved my beard that I had cultivated while at these forward bases, and a haircut was in my plans for that day. My fellow crew chiefs couldn't understand why I wanted to be forward so much, but I did.

I couldn't have been back more than a day or two when Lt. Rich, who was on his way to the airfield, spotted me and asked if I would like to go for a ride. "Bring your M60 with you. We may need it," he shouted. I scurried back to our hooch, grabbed my armored vest, helmet, box of ammo and my M60. The adrenaline rush took over, and I was onboard in minutes and ready to go.

As we lifted off the runway, Lt. Rich keyed his microphone and told me that we were summoned to an area east of the city of Kon Tum. A 4th Division Infantry unit had been ambushed there and four of our boys had been killed. We were to assist in finding the source of the ambush. As we flew away from Camp Enari in our 4th DIVARTY Aviation's OH-23, little did we know what the day would bring. Most bad days started out pretty good for some unknown reason, and you just had to trust your brothers to keep you safe.

I remember the warmth of the morning began to slowly cool down as we gained altitude and followed Highway 19 to our destination. The mountains seemed much like those back home in New York State. The biggest difference was that someone wasn't trying to kill me back there. Our mission was simple (famous last words): pick up an FAC (Forward Air Controller), locate the guilty NVA, and find a landing zone for American-made artillery rounds. The final step of this mission was to provide a death sentence to those responsible for the deaths of these four young men from Anytown, USA.

As we landed to welcome aboard the FAC, our helicopter's rotor wash lifted the green ponchos to reveal the faces of four young men who someday would adorn a granite wall in our nation's capital. As I stared at these brave but lifeless men, I did not realize that this image would remain with me forever. This wasn't the first time I saw a dead GI. It just seemed like it.

It just wasn't right that I knew they were gone before their families were informed. I pictured their families at Sunday dinner reading their letters and how their sons would be home soon. *Don't worry, Mom, Dad. I'll be home soon. Love, your son, John.* I could visualize

Johnny's mother collapsing onto the floor, devoured by uncontrollable horror and praying to God that it can't be true, that there must be some kind of mistake. "Oh, my God!" would be repeated time and time again as the news of Johnny's death spread like wildfire across Anytown, USA. Pastors, neighbors and friends would wear a path to the door to express their heartfelt sympathies. Others wouldn't visit at all, or at least the first couple of days because they didn't know how to act. What could I possibly say that would comfort them? Tears would flow for days as close friends stopped in or called to comfort Johnny's mother. Brothers and sisters would sob and cry out for Johnny. Their brother, who chose to serve his country and looked so handsome in his uniform, was leaving for a faraway place never to return. It was likely that one of the siblings who was too busy to see Johnny off to the airport that day would deeply regret not having that day to do all over again—never to admit the guilt of saying, "I'm just too busy," or "Have a good trip," or "Be careful," and "See you next year."

Memories would surface for years: Remember when Johnny fell out of the tree, broke Mrs. Baker's window and so on. Ooh, Johnny loved to fish in Old Man Dracup's farm pond. He would spend hours bouncing baseballs off the side of the garage, fine-tuning his baseball skills and preparing for his career with his favorite baseball team. The stories would be endless, but the final chapter was just that—final. Johnny wasn't coming home.

The FAC climbed aboard and belted up, and as we lifted off I noticed the four bodies were being covered again. A helicopter was on its way to pick them up for processing and getting them to their not yet informed families. How many more families would experience and survive this terrible life-changing event before it was over? As it turned out, we know now that over 58,000 families would be forced to live out this nightmare.

The microphone in the FAC's helmet could listen but couldn't transmit, so we swapped helmets. Being that he would be calling in the artillery rounds, a fully operational helmet was essential to our success. The helmet swap would soon play a big part in how this day would end. Because of the helmet swap, the pilot and I would have to use hand signals. I placed my hand on the pilot's knee and squeezed his leg to hold and release my grip to move forward. As we drifted down the tree line, the objective was to locate the culprits. If the enemy thought they could get away with it, they might take a shot at this slow-moving helicopter and its occupants, including "Yours truly." The objective was to locate by sight or by drawing fire in order to reveal the enemy's position so that our artillery and gunships could do what they do best.

About two hundred yards down the tree line I squeezed the pilot's leg to slow down. Something caught my eye as I squinted through and around the heavy foliage in the canopy of heavy leaf-laden trees. My eyes locked on another set of eyes looking back at me. An NVA regular leaning against tree made no attempt to raise his AK 47 in my direction. What seemed like minutes was probably but a few seconds. He had the drop on us but seemed uninterested in engaging our OH-23. My M60 was ready to fire, but I kept it pointed away. The battle worn soldier slowly turned and walked away, therefore posing no threat to our safety. I wondered if he had had enough of war and just wanted to go home like everybody else. As I lessened my grip we slowly crept forward.

While this engagement was taking place, I was squeezing the blood out of the pilot's leg with my grip. He keyed up as we drifted another few hundred yards down the tree line. I leaned over to him, as my microphone was still inoperable and he said, "What was that all about?"

"I'll tell you later," I shouted.

At that very moment two bullets ripped through the skids and another through the bubble, exiting behind me where I had just been sitting upright moments before. The pilot pitched the OH-23 forward and to the left to vacate the danger zone. I turned my M60 toward the area I suspected the shooter might be. I continued firing as Lt. Rich applied throttle and flew to a safe distance. I almost emptied my ammo box in the direction of the woods with no proof of my fire finding the guilty culprit who had put holes in our ship.

The FAC had the coordinates ready to go, and in moments 8" Howitzer rounds were dispatched to the woods and all Hell broke loose. The incoming rounds sounded like a herd of screaming freight trains. Observing from a safe distance, we watched as UH1C Huey helicopter gunships made their approach with their death-dealing mini-guns, rockets and door-gunner M60s doing what they do best.

Having been with a gunship company just a couple months ago, I knew what these armed assault machines were capable of, and I felt a little sad that I wasn't in on it. The gunships were equipped with about a dozen 2.75 rockets and two mini-guns that were capable of 2200 rounds a minute with the two door gunners adding another 1000 more. The gunships received return fire, and it was determined that this enemy force was larger than previously thought. A stronger response was therefore necessary. The gunships exited the area to re-arm and refuel and then were replaced with Phantom Air Force jets dropping 500 lb bombs and napalm. The instant heat of the napalm jell blast could be felt well over a half mile away. Artillery rounds were next up, and as always it was quite the display of accuracy and destruction. The woods that once looked like a great place to go camping someday now looked like a wasteland.

Our job was done, and after we refuel we will head back to the safety of Camp Enari. We first must drop the FAC back where we found him. As we settled down to let the FAC out, I couldn't help but notice that the four GI's were now in black body bags and would soon be on their journey home. It wasn't the way they had planned on getting home.

On our way to refuel we noticed a lot of black smoke ahead of us. Having my operational helmet back made communication much easier. We remained silent as we flew over a field that was covered with dead enemy soldiers. *Why the black smoke?* I quickly found out why. The South Vietnamese soldiers were burning NVA bodies. What made it unusual was that they put their dead counterparts in strange positions. Some were posed like they were doing push-ups with sticks under their lifeless chins holding their heads high. Then they doused them with diesel fuel and set them afire. I wasn't quite twenty-one-years old yet, and witnessing this seemed too much for this New York State boy to absorb.

Neither Lt. Rich nor I spoke a word as we flew over the slaughtered and incinerated corpses—not a single word or the slightest hint of what we had just seen. For that matter, Lt. Rich and I seldom discussed anything we did or saw. In about three weeks it would be Lt. Rich who would give this soon to be twenty-one-year-old over fifty years of bonus time.

With the temporary fuel depot in sight, Lt. Rich skillfully and safely placed our craft on ground. With magnetos turned off, the blades that had been rotating for some time slowly came to rest. The never-to-be forgotten smell of burned corpses was stronger here as off to the east the black smoke rose steadily. I couldn't erase the image of the dead enemy soldiers—boys like us, doing push-ups while on fire.

I unbuckled and lifted off my helmet. As I stepped on the ground, my feet were treated with a loud, audible crack. At first, I thought it was a piece of glass, a dinner plate or something ceramic. When I finished the re-fuel and stepped on the skid, I looked down to see what I had stepped on. It was a bald, human skull. The U.S. Army had chosen to place this fuel depot on a mass grave with hundreds of NVA soldiers beneath my feet. What a fitting end for a very long day that I can still see, hear and smell to this day.

The flight back to Camp Enari was uneventful. It was much cooler, and I thought I should have brought a jacket with me. But as we dropped in elevation the temperature rose, making me forget the jacket thing. Lt. Rich was an excellent pilot, and I always felt safe with him on the stick. Another perfect landing and we were home. Well, it was home for now, never to be confused with real home.

As I bedded our OH-23 down for the night, I looked at the bullet holes made hours earlier and realized that of all of the events that took place that day the bullets were almost forgotten. I patched the bullet holes with green Army tape, completed the log book and called it a day. It was a day I would relive quite often. I tied the rotor down, checked the oil, made notes in the log book and made my way to the mess hall. I was starving.

Chapter 14

APRIL 1968

It's 1957, Jamestown, New York. My friends David Henry, Alan Macintyre, and I are playing Army. I've been ambushed behind Mrs. Reed's garage. I fall to the ground wincing in pain. In a few moments I'll get up and it will be my turn to be victorious. We are three ten-year-old boys acting out a scene from a John Wayne or Audie Murphy movie. But it doesn't work that way here in Vietnam! It's real, it's permanent, and you can lose your turn in the blink of an eye.

~~~~

Firebase 14, Kon Tum Province, Central Highlands, Republic of South Vietnam. I'm still here, still alive. I looked at my calendar this morning and it's April 4, 1968. I have 106 days remaining before my trip home. The double-digit fidget was a mere 7 days away. This day was a beauty—perfect sunrise, perfect temperature, and no flights on tap. I stopped by Lt. Rich's tent to make sure it was OK to go into the city of Kon Tum. Drew Taylor and I were going to get some new camouflage fatigues made and then head for the Dak Bla River to go swimming. Lt. Rich said to go ahead and to have a good time.

Drew Taylor and I found a mess tent nearby, and after a plate of something that resembled eggs and spam (at least that's what I thought it was) we headed across the makeshift helipad toward downtown Kon Tum. I quickly noticed my helicopter that was absent from its location where I had done the daily pre-flight only a couple of hours ago. As we got closer I saw a Lt. Noname (pilot) getting ready to disembark in another aircraft. I ran over to him and asked him where Lt. Rich and the OH23 had gone.

"Lt. Rich taxied a Major out to Firebase 14, a few kilometers west of here. When they got ready to leave, the craft sputtered, stalled, and then refused to restart. Magneto failure, I suspect. I'm going to pick up the Major now."

Another soldier climbing aboard is apparently going to stay with Lt. Rich until they either got the 23 started or it was hooked and returned to Camp Enari by a CH 47. I told Lt. Noname that it was my aircraft and my pilot, and therefore I should be the one going to FB 14. The soldier quickly unbuckled, gave me his flak vest, helmet and rifle and seemed to be relieved that I was going and he wasn't.

The sun was clearly at about the 1000 hours in the sky and its warmth was evident as we lifted off. I waved goodbye to Drew, watched him continue his journey to downtown and quickly turned my focus to the direction of the firebase. The no-start problem, although not common, had happened once before, so with that experience under my belt I'm sure we'd be returning shortly.

On the way there two things happened. I was thinking how familiar and beautiful the Central Highlands were and how they resembled the mountain region of my home state of New York. That thought was quickly interrupted when the nameless pilot keyed his microphone and advised me that Firebase 14 was under attack. We best be careful and get out of as soon as possible. Honestly, that didn't faze me at all. Young and still invincible, what could go wrong? Good advice nonetheless.

A distant barren hilltop rapidly came into view as we sped along at just shy of 80 knots (approximately 90 mph). I saw my 23, Lt. Rich and what was no doubt Lt. Rich's taxi fare awaiting our arrival. It seemed a little warmer now, and the sun, although still up there, was partially blocked by the swirling dust of the 23's rotor rotating as the collective stick was raised. This allowed us to land softly on this god-forsaken barren hilltop that must have some importance. Otherwise, why would we be there?

I couldn't get out of the 23's seat quick enough as the Major was chomping at the bit to replace me and get the Hell out of there. Lt.

Rich was pretty anxious to leave as well, but we first had to figure out why this OH-23 wouldn't start. Lt. Rich, who always seemed so calm, had a sense of urgency in his voice while explaining the symptoms of the no-starting aircraft that should and would get us off this place if operational. I immediately unclipped the electrical box located behind the passenger seat. At that same moment I heard the familiar sound of mortar tubes making that oh so familiar thumping sound as they left their tubes en route to our location.

Lt. Rich and I made a dash to a nearby bunker as explosion after explosion landed in the center of the firebase, creating a series of loud impacts and plenty of shrapnel and debris showering us and our aircraft.

In the safety of the bunker, we waited for the intermission of the attack. Once we felt a pause was in place, we ran back to our 23. It appeared our craft was not damaged, so I immediately proceeded with my inspection of the electrical box, looking for the culprit of our extended and unwanted stay at Firebase 14.

Why this even mattered, but I noticed the once warm bright sun had disappeared under a cloud or maybe it was the cloak of dirt and dust from multiple explosions. I could clearly smell the acrid odor of exploded ordnances with which I had been all too familiar in my experiences at Dak To, just a few kilometers north of us.

As if on cue, Lt. Rich and I made a mad dash to our recently visited bunker as the arrival of mortars and now rockets made yet another appearance on this barren and now pock-marked hilltop. This barrage was answered swiftly by Air Force jets, artillery and helicopter gunships.

Thinking this was an opportunity to resume repairs, we scurried to the 23 and again noticed, with the exception of a few holes in the fuselage, that we had sustained limited damage. Our peace and quiet didn't last but five minutes, however, and we were off running for safety once again. Between their exploding rounds and our counterattacks it seemed like the world was coming to an end.

I don't recall how many times we repeated this dash for safety, but it was getting pretty old. Now dirty, sweaty, tired, hungry and thirsty, I could only imagine getting out of this nightmare in the making. What's more, I could hear the unmistaken sound of a Quad 50 caliber machine gun and the rattling of small firearms on the north perimeter of the firebase. It was time to get desperate and find a way out of here.

With another pause in the action, I resumed looking for the cause of being stuck here for all of four hours of having this bullseye on our backs. Lt. Rich, now in the 23, was awaiting my signal to ignite the magnetos that would fire the motor, turn the rotors and lift us to safety, a meal, drink and a shower. The broken porcelain insulator loomed large as I realized it was the same part that created a no-start on another 23 just a few weeks ago in Dak To.

I found and stole a heavy-gauge wire from the lighting system and prepared a jumper wire that would bypass the insulator and fire the magnetos. Once fired, they would stay fired until we landed back at the makeshift airfield at Kon Tum. As I leaned forward to give Lt. Rich the thumbs up to hit the starter, an explosion at the rear of the 23 pushed me forward with great force. An instant later as I was again moving in the direction of the bunker, the ground behind me exploded, driving me forward at a high rate of speed and driving my face into the ground and filling my mouth with Vietnam soil. I now know what Firebase 14 tastes like. A warm sensation took over as blood turned my dirty green Army uniform pant leg blood red—my blood. I felt a deep burning sensation in my lower body and my eyes felt weak as I sensed shock was setting in. I felt my eyes rolling back in my head, a feeling that I can recall to this day. I asked God, "Please, not today."

Lt. Rich was nowhere to be seen, and I suspected he was in the same boat as I was in. Moments passed as I became numb and unable to move. I looked in the direction of the bunker, and there was Lt. Rich going out of sight as he dipped below ground level to safety. A split second later he reappeared, realizing that I wasn't close behind. Then he looked at me, and I remember precisely his look of shock as he saw me lying face down in the dirt and crimson-stained earth around me. It seemed like only a few seconds later he grabbed me by under the armpits and proceeded to drag me to the bunker. He said repeatedly, "I got you . . . you'll be OK."

Inside the bunker the medics worked to stop the bleeding in my right leg. Fully conscious and coherent now, I watched as they applied pressure to my wounds. I don't recall what the medics looked like or anything they said, but I can see Lt. Rich looking on with a sadness that took over his normally calm demeanor. I felt cold and dirty. I didn't know how bad it was, but I was now feeling tired as whatever they gave me in that syringe was beginning to work.

Something kept catching me out of the corner of my left eye. I freed my hand from my side and touched something. It was a long piece of metal sticking out of my cheek below my eye. I recognized it as part of the aircraft. It was an eight-inch piece of metal sticking out of my face. Really? I grabbed hold of it, pulled it out, held it up, and showed it to the medic who didn't seem to care as they were focused on bigger problems. I pulled another piece from my chin and felt myself getting weak and numb. I looked around and saw them carry another soldier into the bunker. His hand was badly damaged, and he was directing them to his chest area where his blood-stained flak vest was showing yet another wound. The medics turned me over and dressed the wound on my back and buttocks while another medic gave aid to the other young soldier.

I strained to look at the damage done by the enemy's 81 mm mortar, hoping to see my leg intact the same as it was only minutes before. As I'm viewing the medics doing their best to make me comfortable, I couldn't help but hear the explosions of incoming mortar, rockets, and our deadly response with artillery and other deadly ordnances.

A medevac helicopter had been summoned to transport me and another soldier to an aid station (MASH). Only a few short months ago at Dak To I witnessed three medevac helicopters shot down as they were removing the wounded to safety. The NVA soldiers wouldn't shoot the Huey with a big Red Cross painted on its fuselage when it was arriving. Instead, they'd wait until the wounded were aboard, and on the departure they would open fire.

The medic relayed the message from the radioman that the medvac was near and it was time to go. As the stretcher bearers prepared me for the dash to the helipad and the incoming rescue ship, I could only think about those who met their demise at the point when they thought they were safe from harm and heading home soon. I was scared like never before as I lay there waiting to depart.

I was loaded on quickly and carefully, which afforded me no opportunity to say goodbye to Lt. Rich. The all too familiar sound of the Huey's engine whining and building rpms for takeoff was overshadowed by the thought of bullets tearing through the paper-thin floors and finishing what my adversaries had set out to do in the first place.

"We'll have you home in no time," the crew chief yelled over the noise of the now ascending med-e-vac helicopter. I braced myself, fearing the worst. Firebase 14 was still under attack, but as we quickly flew away my fear subsided. I could feel and hear my heartbeat as I do at this very moment of writing. I caught the eye of the crew chief and asked him where they were taking me. "Dak To," he replied. "Seriously?" I said to myself. One of the most dangerous places on earth and you're taking me there? The crew chief sensed my concern. Then he said, "They'll clean your wounds and send you to the 71st EVAC Hospital in Pleiku. You're going home."

The sun was shining through the glass in the sliding door of the Huey as I felt us descending. The pilot gently landed near the aid station, and the other wounded young soldier and I were whisked away to the aid station. It would be my last visit to Dak To. Dak To was and will forever be a place that harbors so many memories for me.

I remember a nurse, maybe two nurses started cutting my blood-soaked fatigues, socks and boots off me while a doctor and a nurse rolled me over and surveyed and dressed my wounds. A young black soldier lay next to me, and I could see he was missing a leg. I didn't know it then, but we would be side by side again in a holding area later waiting for a ride to the 71st EVAC Hospital in Pleiku. He was wounded by artillery, a victim of friendly fire.

It must be late afternoon, I thought. I know now that I was wounded and medevac'd about 1130 hours. Whatever they gave me made me very sleepy, and I don't remember anything until I woke up in new surroundings sometime in the early evening. The opportunity didn't present itself to thank Lt. Rich for risking his life until forty years later. I had found him through a veteran's locater service run by a Vietnam vet from Corning, New York. When he answered the phone I said, "Is this Rich? This is Mick. I'm so glad I found you." As I spoke, I choked back my tears and felt the lump in my throat getting bigger by the moment.

"I knew it was you and I knew we'd talk someday," he said. I struggled to get the words out as my speech slurred out the words, "Thank you for saving my life."

"You are welcome." Then he broke into laughter. "This is amazing," he said. "I just told the rat story a few days ago. Capt. Broyer never did talk to me again." For the next hour, Lt. Rich and I talked about what we had done over those forty years. Finally, running out of things to say, I thanked him once more and we said goodbye. The weight of finding him and thanking him was finally lifted off my shoulders.

I lingered in a drug-induced slumber until I reached the 71st EVAC Hospital in Pleiku. Darkness was closing in, and I couldn't have been in my bed but for a short spell when a very large nurse from

Alabama informed me that she didn't care if I was a General. "In this ward I'm boss and you ain't nothing," she barked. "You'll do as I say and when I say it." I was in no shape to argue. Within a few minutes I was hauled off to an operating room where two surgeons commenced to operate on me. I was given a sedative—a spinal injection—and I felt nothing but heard everything.

One of the doctors said to the other, "This guy's going to have a problem getting through metal detectors."

The masked surgeon looked at me and said, "We are going to leave most of this metal in you. If we take it all out, you won't have much of a leg left. We got the big pieces and what look like shards of aircraft sheet metal out. You're going home, soldier!"

My nurse—I'll call her Ms. Alabama—had food waiting for me as they wheeled me back to my spot. "Rest up today, honey, 'cuz tomorrow I'll have you on your feet. Who's Boss here?" I answered, "You are." The rest of the day was watching and listening to all these boys moaning, groaning and some crying at what wound they had been dealt. Only God knows what dinner was, but it wasn't long after that last bite that an all too familiar sound of a mortar round impacting the ground overshadowed the groans. Ms. Alabama appeared out of nowhere, shouting for us to get out of bed and get on the floor. I tried to move, but I was hooked up to tubes, wires and a sheet tucked in too tight. Ms. Alabama darted to my bed, disconnected my stuff, picked me up, laid me on the floor, grabbed my mattress, covered me with it and said, like she meant it, "Boy, you stay under that mattress until I come get you, you hear me?" Who was I to disobey the Boss? Mortars and rockets were exploding, sirens blaring and our defenses were firing back at a greater rate than what was incoming. Fifteen minutes later all was quiet, no direct hits on our ward, not sure about anyone else. Ms. Alabama, as promised, helped me back into my bed.

Two days later I was being prepared for my next stop at Cam Rahn Bay and then off to a U.S. hospital at Tachikowa Airbase, Japan. As they wheeled me out on a stretcher, I spotted Ms. Alabama. I threw her a kiss. God blessed her and thanked her for everything. As they readied us to load on a C-130, she walked by, tugged my green Army blanket and winked. As I lay there waiting for takeoff, I felt something near my stomach. I lifted the blanket and, low and behold, a Hershey candy bar. Ms. Alabama—what a lady!

A one-night stay in Cam Rahn Bay was all that was needed. I don't recall much of that stay at all. The next morning, we were placed on an Air Force jet and transported to the U.S. military hospital at Tachikowa Air Base in Japan. This place is beautiful in every way—the facility, the care, beautiful nurses, and safe. I would spend three weeks there going through a painful rehab. My Achilles' tendon had been damaged and would cause me unbelievable pain while rehabbing. I was bed-ridden for the first nine days. The food was pretty good, but I heard of this great food at the mess hall and looked forward to going there.

In the bed next to me was a young black Marine from Georgia. Half of his face was heavily bandaged. He was all tubed up, and nurses and doctors attended to him around the clock. He had arrived there a few days before me. About a week later he would become alert and talkative. His wounds were caused by an NVA artillery round causing extensive damage to his right side, but the worst was the loss of his right eye. After a few days of cordial conversation, I got up the nerve and asked him, "How do you feel about the loss of your eye?" A minute or two went by before I received a reply I never expected. He looked at me and pointed to his remaining eye and said, "I'm so glad I still have this one." The one thing all veterans shared—Black or White—was that our blood was red . . . American red.

≈≈≈

Growing up in the little, and I mean little town of Sanborn, New York, had its advantages. First, you know everyone. Second, when the firehall sounded its siren, you knew it was noon. Finally, everyone knew Charlie Treichler. Charlie and I have baby pictures together. We played Little League baseball and we played Army soldier. Charlie lived next door to my grandparents, and when I would spend summers there, we hung out.

I was on convoy duty in August, 1967. I received a letter from Grandma a couple of days earlier that Charlie was in a place called the Oasis. When we arrived, I realized this firebase was larger than I expected, and the needle in a haystack quandary came to mind. While they were unloading my truck, I thought I'd wander around to check this place out. I come to a dirt cross road. Trust me, this was not any kind of intersection you would know. I stood there for a moment, when as I was about to light up a smoke, someone shouted out my name: "Hey, Paul."

I stopped the smoke lighting procedure, and I looked up at a truck in front of me, and there was Charlie peering down at me. From that point on, anytime I was at the Oasis or Charlie was at Camp Enari we would hang out.

Moving ahead, I'm in the hospital in Japan, 2500 miles from Camp Enari. A Marine from Hawaii was wheel-chairing me to the mess hall. We were rolling along nicely headed for breakfast when all of a sudden my Marine buddy was walking along side me and I was still moving. I turned to see who was pushing me and guess who? Charlie! Walking behind Charlie were a male and a female nurse. I didn't pay much attention at the time, but they were from the mental health section of Tachikowa. I didn't see Charlie for a couple of days until one afternoon while I was having lunch with my Marine buddy, I noticed Charlie at a distance. Seated with him were two orderlies and a young doctor.

The doctor stood up, walked to my table, sat down, and asked me where I was from. "New York," I said. "Why do you ask?"

"What town?" I sensed it had something to do with Charlie, so I said, "Sanborn."

The doctor seemed shocked. "Charlie has been telling us for days that someone he grew up with was here." The doctor went on to tell me that Charlie had been having some issues.

"We never know what to believe as he often slips away from us, if you know what I mean. My God, Paul, would it be OK with you if we gave Charlie permission to visit you and take you around in your wheelchair? It would do him wonders."

"Of course," I said. So, it turned out that every day Charlie would wheel me to breakfast, lunch and dinner, providing he wasn't in what he called "a session."

A couple of weeks later I received word I would be going Stateside. I broke the news to a disappointed Charlie. That night at dinner the young doctor I had talked to came to my table.

"Paul, you'll never know what it meant to Charlie seeing you here." The doctor went on to say that when Charlie first told us about you, we figured it was just another one of his imaginary friends. "Thank you for letting Charlie interact with you. His road to recovery leaped forward tenfold. We'll be sending him home soon."

In a month or more I would get a convalescent leave from the Army hospital in Ft. Devens, Massachusetts. I went to Sanborn after a few days in Rochester to visit my two favorite human beings—Gramps and Gramma. As I stepped out of the car, I looked down the street toward the old fire hall and saw the silhouette of a young man walking toward me on the shoulder of Ward Road. I stood on the driveway and slowly watched as the silhouette slowly and clearly came into view. It was Charlie. A handshake and a chest bump signaled that we both made it home. Charlie's wounds were deeper than mine and would last forever. In that regard, I was the lucky one.

The trip home to the States on a stretcher was what you might expect. I must have slept most of the way because the first stop seemed like a ten-minute flight to Anchorage, Alaska. The Red Cross couldn't do enough to make our journey more comfortable. They took us off

125

the airplane on our stretchers to an area at the airport and fed us breakfast. We left Anchorage a few hours later, and what we were are about to experience was unexpected. The aircraft landed at McGuire Air Force Base in Maryland.

As the pilot taxied to the terminal he came on the intercom. "Gentlemen, in about three minutes I'm going to open the back of this aircraft. Please be ready." The three minutes passed and the aircraft came to a halt. The noise of the hydraulics and mechanical sounds of the ramp lowering revealed a beautiful, sunny and warm day. As our eyes fixed on this beautiful Maryland morning, the pilot came back on the intercom: "Gentlemen, Welcome Home." After a few moments of dead silence and, as if on cue, the entire aircraft of young soldiers exploded in cheers. "God Bless America" was on everyone's lips, as tears rolled down the cheeks of everyone onboard. As they carried us off the plane, an honor guard on each side of ramp saluted as we passed.

We arrived at the hospital and were no sooner settled in when the Red Cross nurses made their way into the hospital ward stopping at each bed, now mine.

"What would you like to eat?" one of the nurses asked.

"Whatever you have, as long as it's not in a green can," I said jokingly. Trying to be funny, I said, "I'd like a cheeseburger, fries and a vanilla shake."

"Your mother is waiting by the phone in Rochester," said the nurse. "Would you like to talk with her while I get your food?"

It had been almost a year since I spoke to Mom. I talked to Mom, then Dad and all of sudden I felt home. My fifteen minutes of phone time was up, and as I handed the phone back to the nurse a tray appeared with a cheeseburger, fries and a vanilla shake.

The next day we traveled to a military hospital by air to Fort Devens, Massachusetts. My health and mobility would increase tenfold while there. Another soldier and I took in some great sightseeing in and around Boston. I was eager to go home. In a few days, I would take a convalescent leave and finally go home. I never doubted I'd be home again. I wasn't as healthy as when I departed, but I was going home.

Chapter 15

"WELCOME HOME"

A funny thing happened to me when I came home from Vietnam. Nobody asked me where I'd been for the last year, and I never volunteered to tell anyone that I had been there, what I did, or what happened to me.

≈≈≈

You've heard the story before. The American soldier was being held responsible for the war in Vietnam, not the president, not Congress, not the Senate, and not big business that profited. Nope, the American G.I., the twenty-year-old kid from Anytown, USA, was the bad guy. He was ridiculed in public with no welcome home, no parade, no respect, just blame and shame.

My first welcome home was on an airplane coming home from the hospital, but let me give you a little background first. It had been a year since I returned home. I'd spent three months in hospitals in Vietnam, Japan, Maryland and Massachusetts. I finally got the OK to go home on convalescent leave. The Army hospital was located in Fort Devens, Massachusetts, the airport was Boston's Logan International and my ticket was to Rochester (New York) International. Now, Rochester International is kind of a stretch. I think it got the international tag when a Canadian Cessna made an emergency landing in 1956.

I was getting ready to leave for Logan International when my doctor, Capt. Newsome, asked me, "Do you have any civilian clothes?"

"No," I said.

"Well, maybe you should get some," he replied.

"I have my uniform, sir."

"Listen, Paul, Army uniforms can become a target for those who don't necessarily approve of what's going on over there."

"Really? Well, I'm not buying clothes."

"Well, don't say I didn't warn you," he replied while peering over his spectacles.

When I arrived at Logan there were no protesters, but I did get the evil eye from a couple of hippie types. I wasn't worried, but I did feel some kind of relief in that I wasn't being ridiculed or spat upon. I boarded the airplane and took an aisle seat next to a grandfather-aged, white haired man. I'm going to call him Mr. Whipple. Many years later I met a man walking by my house. He would stop and visit every day while I was putting in a new sidewalk. He reminded me of the grandfather on the plane. His name was Mr. Whipple. We struck up a struck up a conversation for about ten minutes on our one-hour flight. He saw my cane, and coupled with the uniform he put two and two together. He was dying to ask, so he did.

"I hope you don't mind, but were you wounded in Vietnam?"

"Yes, I was."

"Are you going home?"

"Yes, for the first time, sir."

"Will your folks be there to meet you?"

"I hope so. It was kind of a short notice." He paused for a few minutes and in a lower voice said, "We lost our grandson over there."

"I'm so sorry, sir," I said as I glanced at this nice old man much like my own grandfather.

"He was an Airborne soldier. He died last November in a place called Dak To."

You could have smacked me with a ton of bricks. "Sir," I said, "I am so sorry, I was there. The 173rd Airborne, right?"

His head turned quickly toward me. "Did you know him?" he asked. "Were you with that unit?"

"No sir, but I do know that the 173rd fought there and fought bravely. I'm so sorry." Our communication ended abruptly as I could see sorrow overtake him.

As the overhead 'FASTEN SEATBELT' sign lit up, the stewardess announced that we were on our final approach. I couldn't see my family yet, but I'm sure they were there someplace. As the aircraft came to a stop, the safety-belt light went off, and I unbuckled my belt. I still tear up when I think of what happened next. Mr. Whipple put his hand on my knee and said, "Welcome home, son! I'm happy for you and your family." He extended his hand. I shook it and said, "Thank you, sir."

I grabbed my carry-on and my cane from the overhead and made my way to the exit. I had a newspaper in hand when I saw my mom, dad, sister Kay and Lori following close behind. I opened the paper to conceal my face, and as they drew near I dropped it. My mother let out a shrill as she saw me. We hugged a long time . . . and I mean a long time. Dad, then Kay, then six-year-old sister Lori repeated the process. My brothers Rod and Scott waited at home so as not to tear up in public. Too real softies! Our home was our next stop, and as we started walking to the exit and our ride home, Mr. Whipple, who had been standing in the background, approached us, introduced himself and first shook my father's hand and then embraced my mother.

"I'm so happy your son made it home. God bless you!" Mr. Whipple turned as he walked away and waved at me and saying, "Welcome home." Other than my family and other Vietnam veterans, it would be fifty years before another meaningful "Welcome home" greeting would come along. I'll get to that shortly. Vietnam veterans don't wear T-shirts and hats to broadcast to the world that they are veterans. They wear them to attract other Vietnam vets.

≈≈≈

It's the year 2017 and I'm returning home to Rochester from Tampa, Florida. My baggage was checked and I had about an hour to kill. I was approaching an escalator when off to my right I spotted a man about my age sporting a Vietnam Veteran hat. I made a hard-right-hand turn, and as I got closer I spoke the magic words: "Welcome home, brother." He quickly replied, "Welcome home, brother." We shook hands and had the normal conversation that included what years we served, our unit, what part of Vietnam where we stationed, and our MOS (Military Occupational Specialty). This wasn't my first conversation with a Vietnam veteran by any stretch. We talked for ten minutes or so before I excused myself from our conversation, shook hands, and we hugged each other while repeating, "Welcome home, brother," something all Vietnam veterans say to one another. I walked toward the escalator, and about halfway up I glanced back at my recently discovered 'brother.' His wife had her arms wrapped tightly around her man as he sobbed uncontrollably. I realized at that very moment that we shared something that no one could possibly understand but us. You can't buy, lease, borrow or appear on some silly reality show to experience what we went through while we were over there and years, and even decades after we got home. So when you see a Vietnam veteran with his hat or T-shirt depicting his service, it's not for you. He's looking for one of his brothers.

The hands down best "Welcome home" would take place one year later. See if you agree. Three friends—Mike Mitchell, Dave Trobia and Mike Judy—and I were golfing in Naples, Florida. We went to an upscale area called Mercato that boasts some pretty high-end restaurants and shops. After our visit to Rocky Patel's Cigar Bar we went to a restaurant close by for dinner. Service was rather poor and our meals came at different times. The two Mike's and I finished and

Dave's meal was sent back. We asked Dave if he would mind if we walked around and we'd meet back at the car.

Being a coffee addict, I recalled seeing a coffee shop called the Second Cup on our way to Rocky Patel's Cigar Bar. One of the Mike's went home, and the other went with me. "I need to get a cup of coffee, Mike." So I walked in. There was one person in line, so I stood there patiently awaiting my turn. I couldn't help but notice the man in front of me was Asian. As he turned I reckoned him to be Vietnamese.

"Excuse me," I said, "are you Vietnamese, sir?"

"Yes, I am."

"How are we treating you here in America?" I asked.

"We love it here," he said. He asked me if I had been in his country during the war, and I said that I had been there a long time ago. He thrust his hand toward me and while shaking my hand he said, "Thank you for what you did for us."

"You're welcome. I wish we could have done more," I said apologetically. He went on to tell me that an American soldier had sponsored his mother and father and brought them to America. The Army soldier gave them a place to live, fed them and clothed them until they could take care of themselves.

"We are very grateful to America and its soldiers," he said compassionately. You would have thought I was that soldier whose kindness made such a difference in their lives.

"Well, you are welcome," I said. He continued to the end of the counter to get his beverages, and I remember thinking what a grateful person he must be that he would take the time to thank me for just being there. I ordered my coffee, paid for it and made my way to the end of the counter. I picked up my coffee, turned to find Mike so we could return to the car. But my path was blocked by the Vietnamese man I had just met, although this time he had with him his wife and his twin daughters. They were a beautiful family, nicely dressed, incredibly polite with two well-disciplined young girls probably in their early teens.

He walked toward me and said, "I would like you to meet my family." He went on to say, "I told them what you did for our country, and we they would like to thank you and welcome you home." He introduced his wife and two daughters to me, and as I hugged and thanked them each for their kindness, a felt a blanket of warmth come over me. The mother of all "Welcome home" greetings was taking place right in front of me . . . and I knew it. I shook the father's hand once more and thanked him once again for his kindness. I looked around for Mike, spotted him at the door, and started walking toward him. I glanced back at that beautiful family as I got to the door. My ear-to-ear smile must have been a dead giveaway.

Mike couldn't wait to ask. "What was that all about?

"I'll tell you about it on the way home," I replied. This "Welcome Home" was special. In talking to hundreds of Vietnam veterans over the years I found that almost to the man the "Welcome Home" meant more coming from another vet. We shared an experience and we performed what was asked of us, but the treatment we received was like no other in our history. Over 58,000 young men and women made the ultimate sacrifice, and now, decades later, they want to thank us? They had their chance to welcome us home fifty-plus-years ago, but they blew it.

EPILOGUE

We must never forget those who died, those who are forever transformed, and those who survived. We must educate our children and our children's children. We must promote the healing that our community and our country were not ready to embrace.

Laura Palmer (Shrapnel in the Heart) 1987

≈≈≈

The Vietnam War took its toll on those young men and women who served. And, of course, their families suffered. More than anything else, however, was its toll on our country. It tore us apart from within, and its critics labeled America's best young men as evil, villains, and worst of all, baby killers. America would pay a dear price in so many ways that to this day remnants of guilt and shame still linger. Nineteen- and twenty-year-old boys, most far away from home for the first time, were thrust into 'kill or be killed' war-zone scenarios only a few months removed from high school. Many Vietnam veterans never recovered from the shame thrust upon them by the very people that they thought they were serving.

The Numbers:

9,087,000 US military served during the Vietnam War era worldwide.

2,709,918 of those served in Vietnam. Of those who served in the Vietnam war, the vast majority were volunteers and not drafted as once thought.

24% (648,500) of total forces in country were draftees.

Draftees accounted for 30.4% (17,725) of combat deaths in Vietnam.

Only 10% of those that were "boots on ground"

Over 58,000 were killed (KIA), 304,000 wounded (WIA), 75,000 severely disabled, 23,214 were 100% disabled, 5,283 lost limbs, and 1,081 sustained multiple amputations.

Of those killed, 61% were younger than 21 years old.

11,465 of those killed were younger than 20 years old.

Of those killed, 17,539 were married.

The average age of the young men killed: 23.1 years old.

Five men killed in Vietnam were only 16-year-old boys.

The youngest serviceman killed, Dan Bullock, was 15 years old. In 2019 a North Carolina State historical marker honoring his life was erected near his childhood home in Goldsboro, N.C.

Most killed were in the Army with 38,209. Most were Killed in Action (KIA) by gunfire.

In World War II there were roughly 40 days of combat to every 4 years of service.

In Vietnam there were 240 days of combat to every 1 year of service!

997 soldiers were killed on their first day in Vietnam.

1,448 soldiers were killed on their last day in Vietnam.

31 sets of brothers are on the Wall.

31 sets of parents lost 2 of their sons.

Total: Over 58,000 soldiers were killed, including men formerly classified as MIA casualties. Men who have subsequently died of wounds account for the changing total.

11,000 women served in Vietnam; 8 who died were nurses. One of the nurses who died was killed by hostile fire—Sharon Lane from Zanesville, Ohio. Post No. 12190 (chartered July 4, 2019) of the Veterans of Foreign Wars of the United States (VFW) at Evans, Georgia, is named after her.

Races (from of the total of 58,200 who served):

- White: 49,830

- African American: 7,243

- Hispanic: 349

- All others: 798

The life expectancy of Assault Helicopter crews was often exaggerated. Nonetheless, it was a dangerous profession to say the least. I believe that Scouts had less of a chance of going home. Scouts were in serious harm's way as they flew along tree lines looking for the enemy at a little faster than a hover and sometimes only twenty or thirty feet above the trees. My closest calls came doing exactly that. Hey, in my twenty-year-old mind I was invincible.

5,086 out of 11,827 helicopters were lost in Vietnam.

2,709 people (including transportees) were killed while in Hueys.

1,074 pilots were killed.

1,103 crew members were killed.

Post War Deaths:

60,000 Vietnam veterans have committed suicide (22 each day). That's more than the total of soldiers who died in the entire war. Let that sink in.

Over 300,000 Vietnam veterans have died as a result of Agent Orange. That number will continue to grow. For every soldier killed in Vietnam, six will perish as a result of Agent Orange and suicide.

61% of the men killed were 21 or younger.

11,465 of those killed were younger than 20 years old.

Of those killed, 17,539 were married

Average age of men killed: 23.1 years old.

Enlisted: 50,274; 22.37 years

Officers: 6,598; 28.43 years

Warrants Officers 1,276; 24.73 years

≈ ≈ ≈

Vietnam veterans represented 9.7% of their generation. They have a lower unemployment rate than the same non-veteran age groups. Their personal income exceeds that of our non-veteran age group by more than 18%. The vast Majority of Americans (87%) hold Vietnam veterans in high esteem. There is no difference in drug usage between Vietnam veterans and non-Vietnam veterans of the same age group (Source: Veterans Administration Study).

Vietnam veterans are less likely to be in prison, i.e., only .005% of Vietnam Veterans have been jailed for crimes.

97% of Vietnam veterans were honorably discharged.

85% of Vietnam veterans made successful transitions into civilian life.

91% of Vietnam veterans say they are glad they served.

74% say they would serve again, even knowing the possible outcome.

As of April 14, 2017, there are 1,611 Americans still unaccounted for from the Vietnam War across Vietnam (1,258), Laos (297), Cambodia (49), and China (7). As of 2020, 58,279 names of those who died are on "The Wall."

As of this writing, it's been almost fifty-three years since that day on Firebase 14, Kon Tum Province, Vietnam. At first, I thought that in putting this life experience on paper I didn't have enough material that would interest anyone. Just the reverse happened. I discovered that as I recalled incidents my memory's vault opened wide, and memories good and bad flowed with ease. The whole premise of this was to show you what our country asked a twenty-year-old boy from Henrietta, New York, to do and how we dealt with the rejection and shame that was waiting for us when we came home.

The Vietnam Wall in our nation's capital is a powerful reminder of that terrible period in our history. Over 58,000 men and 8 women are remembered there. My high school friend, David, and his wife Sharon went to Washington, D.C., a few years ago. I had mentioned to them that they should visit the Wall when there. A few days later I got a phone call from Dave, who shared the following profound experience:

"Sharon and I were leaving the Lincoln Memorial, and knowing that we had to pass by the Wall on the way to the car, I suggested to Sharon that as long as we were here let's see the Vietnam Memorial. Sharon replied sharply, 'When are these guys going to get over this war?'

'Well, we have to go by it anyway, so let's check it out,' Dave said.

Sharon and I walked toward the memorial and started down the path when Sharon arrived at the granite wall with the names over 58,000 soldiers right in front of her. She stopped, dropped to her knees, and wept.

'Oh my God,' she exclaimed. 'I had no idea.' Sharon took the phone from Dave and said, 'Paul, I am so sorry I said what I did. I am so sorry. I have never been so moved by anything like this.'"

I think I've been to the Wall fifteen times, maybe more, and it's emotional each and every time. I've witnessed many people like Sharon at the Wall. I took my niece's two boys there a few years ago. The younger boy, Luke, was six, maybe seven at the time. My wife, Carol, explained to Luke what the Wall represented. Luke looked at all the names as we made our way out toward the Lincoln Memorial. That was when Luke grabbed my hand and said, "Uncle Paul, I'm glad you're not on that wall. I said, "Me too."

President Richard M. Nixon once said, "Let me make myself perfectly clear." So, let me make *myself* perfectly clear: I don't profess to be a war hero or someone who did more than the next. I did what was asked of me, and somehow I felt inclined to do a little more, but it was not a fraction of what so many did before and after me.

When veterans were asked, 74% said they would serve again.

Of those discharged, 97% hold an honorable discharge.

The unemployment rate for Vietnam War Veterans was 4.8% compared to 6.2% for the rest of the country.

85% of the Vietnam War veterans made a successful transition to civilian life.

74% said they would serve again even knowing the possible outcome.

The Brotherhood:

The special bond that all Vietnam veterans share is so strong, so powerful that unless you experience it, feel it, and live it, you'll never understand it. We'll cross streets, parking lots, grocery stores, and airport terminals to welcome a brother home. We'll take time to share our units, location and timelines. It's not unusual to prolong a handshake, a hug or an extended conversation with a total stranger. A welcome home from another vet is a sincere heartfelt show of solidarity and respect. We all to the man agree that we were asked to perform our duty and we did. The pain and suffering we saw and experienced can't be bought, rented or duplicated by any ridiculous reality show. The sorrow for those lost and for those who suffer the effects of PTSD and the effects of Agent Orange is real.

I don't know of any combat veteran who refused to admit to mentally blocking what we did, how we did it and the memory loss acquired when we come home. I was suffering amnesia, and I had been told by family members and friends that when I returned and when asked to share experiences, I would give a blank stare and turn on my deaf ears. I didn't know how to answer. I didn't know what they wanted to hear, so I said nothing. Before this writing, I shared my experiences of the horrors of war only with other veterans. We welcome each other home, we shed tears for those lost, and honor those still living.

PTSD Symptoms:

• Feeling upset by things that remind you of what happened;

• Having nightmares, vivid memories, or flashbacks of the event that make you feel like it's happening all over again;

• Feeling emotionally cut off from others;

• Feeling numb or losing interest in things you used to care about;

• Feeling constantly on guard;

• Feeling irritated or having angry outbursts;

• Having difficulty sleeping;

• Having trouble concentrating; and

• Being jumpy or easily startled.

Don't kid yourself. PTSD lives. It's real in every way. There are different levels of PTSD, and it rears its ugly head at the most unpredictable times. It's always there, and out of nowhere something you see, hear or say triggers it. If I see a commercial of a GI coming home surprising his family or a YouTube video of something similar, I can't swallow with that baseball-sized lump in my throat. On a scale of 1 to 10, I would put myself at a 6 or 7 for PTSD, but nowhere near what I've seen at focus groups.

POSTSCRIPT

Age is catching up to us. Each day 390 Vietnam veterans die. By 2025 there won't be a lot of us remaining. So, I hope history treats us fairly.

Hero is one of the most overused words in our vocabulary. I just happen to know where you can view about 58,000 heroes—the Wall in Washington, D.C. That's where you'll find them, all in one place.

Various and numerous public sources provided the above statistics. If you are a Vietnam veteran, "Welcome home, brother." If you are a non-combat or peacetime veteran, I thank you for your service and support.

SPECIAL NOTE

STOLEN VALOR

*S*tolen valor describes the behavior of military impostors, i.e., the act by individuals who falsely claim military service and a rank not earned. Nothing infuriates a Vietnam veteran more than one of these losers. I have run across them numerous times. They are easy to smoke out as they often have vague answers to questions about their alleged military service. For example, when questioned about when they served, under which unit, or their MOS designation, the imposter would reply with responses that clearly rang false and fraudulent.

Recently, I was passing through our workplace cafe and spotted a man wearing a 'Vietnam Veteran' hat. As always, I approached and offered a "Welcome Home, Brother." Almost every time there is a hesitation and a lackluster "You too" or very weak "Welcome home" with the omission of "Brother." I took this man to task with a few questions about his military service. When I asked him when he was there and where he was stationed, he replied "late 60s and all over."

"What was your MOS?" I asked.

"I was a mechanic," he answered.

"Oh," said I. "Helicopter, truck, heavy equipment?" I glanced at his wife sitting next to him and sensed she knew the gig was up.

I didn't let up. "Don't you think it odd that you didn't know where you were, what you did and when you did it?" I stood up, made sure he was looking at me, and I said, "You need to take that hat off." He offered no defense, no rebuttal to my comments and quickly turned the other direction. I walked away, and ten minutes later when I passed through the café, he was gone. He was but one of many impostors I have encountered over the years.

On June 3, 2013 President Barack Obama signed into law the American Legion-backed Stolen Valor Act of 2013, which now makes it a "federal crime for an individual to fraudulently hold oneself out to be a recipient of any of several specified military decorations or medals with the intent to obtain money, property, or other tangible benefit." Taking credit for something that many gave life and limb for just isn't right. Ask a Vietnam vet. He'll tell you.

ACKNOWLEDGEMENTS

First, I wish to thank my parents Helen and Paul. I never had to go without a meal, a roof over my head or a place called home. Four sisters and two brothers made growing up so much fun and always pretty interesting. My grandparents Roy and Nettie were the ones who showed me the right paths to take and the right way to get there. Aunts, uncles, and cousins contributed to putting the pieces of my life's puzzle together.

Thank you, especially to Dr. Pete who inspired me to write this memoir. About seven or eight years ago my amnesia began to wear off and certain events in this memoir began to rear their ugly heads. A golfing buddy who was also a Vietnam vet suggested I meet with a physician at the Veterans Center here in Rochester, New York. I met with A. Peter Ziarnowski, Ph.D. Rochester Vet Center. After a few visits Dr. Pete, as we call him, asked me to write about my experiences. I did just that and began to feel a release of feelings that I had long denied. A few years went by, and one day I found some of those experiences and recollections that I had noted on a yellow legal pad I had tucked away. From those memories I began composing my memoir, touching up the details of those early memories and sharing them with friends and my wife Carol. Now I share them with you.

I am, of course, deeply grateful to my wife of thirty years, Carol, who endured my ignoring her while writing this memoir. She recently passed away and will never see the finished product. I thank her for encouraging me to write my book and see it through. My apologies to my son, Jason, for not having shared all of these events. I hope that he appreciates the gravity of this memoir and what it means to me. Next, let me express my gratitude to my editor and high school friend, Gary Klinga, who gave me the direction and encouragement to put this chapter of my life on paper. Also, special thanks go out to Emma Saunders for her fine image editing work and Sam Villareale (Villastrations@gmail.com) for his fine cover illustration. My

146

gratitude also goes out to Stanley Thornton, publisher at Mystic Dragon Publishing, for helping to produce an affordable book for readers to enjoy and for making it come alive in real form. I also wish to extend my thanks to Betty Judy for her assistance and encouragement in producing my memoir.

Finally, my inspiration to write my experiences shared in the book stems from a brotherhood that I share with thousands of young boys like me who were sent off to a faraway place to fight a war that left an emptiness in the soul of America. Those of us that returned left bits and pieces of our youth behind and came home unwelcome. Many are still dying from disease and sorrow. I, like many, wonder *What was it all about and how did we get there?* Regrettably, there are no simple answers to those questions in the memoir, just my story.

I trust that after reading *Once a Boy,* those of you who are friends will remain friends. When you see one of those guys wearing their Vietnam cap or T-shirt, take a moment and think of him kindly. You will know what to do next.

Help Us Give Smiles

HUGS

FOUNDATION, INC.

In 2011 I went to Hanoi, Vietnam, with Dr. Vito Quatela to perform a site visit of the hospital where HUGS would be performing their life-changing surgeries on children and young adults. Dr. Quatela, president and founder, arrived at a point in his life where he wanted to use his skills to impact the lives of children around the world. Driven by that simple yet profound goal, in 2003 Dr. Quatela established the HUGS Foundation, Inc. (Help Us Give Smiles). Since then, he has recruited a team of skilled surgeons who donate their time and services to correcting congenital facial deformities for children in underserved countries around the world.

Dr. Q, as he is affectionately called, gave me an opportunity to give a little back to the world to which I owe so much. I joined his foundation in 2006 as a board member with the responsibility of organizing fund-raising events and increasing public awareness of the HUGS Foundation.

Visiting Hanoi was a short but meaningful trip, to say the least. Dr. Q would often introduce me as a Vietnam veteran. I was always received with warmth and kindness by everyone I met. Hanoi is a unique and beautiful city, and I would highly recommend a visit. The future of HUGS is bright and Dr. Quatela has plans to double missions in the future. The purchase of *Once a Boy* already provides a donation to The HUGS Foundation. If you wish to make an additional donation to HUGS, I will send you another book as a gift for your kindness. You can also donate on the HUGS website.

https://helpusgivesmiles.org/

149

ABOUT THE AUTHOR

Paul Gardner hails from Western New York State. He was born in Sanborn, New York, and raised in North Tonawanda, Jamestown and Henrietta (Rochester). After his discharge from the Army in 1969, Paul came home and then in 1974 moved to Phoenix, Arizona, residing there for five years followed by three years in Oregon. He retired from the automobile sales business after forty years and now enjoys gardening, woodworking, golf and fly fishing. Exploring America is his passion.

Charitable organizations have been a main focus of his life for over forty-five years. Once the Arizona State Director of the Cystic Fibrosis Foundation and currently an active member of the HUGS Foundation in Rochester keep him aligned with reality and the opportunity to give back. If you ever wanted to understand PTSD, then read the book! Over fifty thousand words of the memoir have been locked up in his brain's file cabinet for over fifty years waiting to escape. Paul hopes that after reading this memoir you will have a greater understanding of what our country asked us boys to do.

My contact email address: onceaboy83@gmail.com.

Made in United States
North Haven, CT
06 February 2023

32079652R00105